For Love's Sake

For Love's Sake

*One Young Woman's Trek With the World's Poor
and Your Open Door to a Life of Experiential Love*

Jessica J. Davis

DESTINY IMAGE® PUBLISHERS, INC.

P.O. Box 310, Shippensburg, PA 17257-0310

"Speaking to the Purposes of God for This Generation and for the Generations to Come."

This book and all other Destiny Image, Revival Press, MercyPlace, Fresh Bread, Destiny Image Fiction, and Treasure House books are available at Christian bookstores and distributors worldwide.

For a U.S. bookstore nearest you, call 1-800-722-6774.

For more information on foreign distributors, call 717-532-3040.

Reach us on the Internet: www.destinyimage.com.

ISBN 13 Trade Paper: 978-0-7684-3680-8

ISBN 13 Hardcover: 978-0-7684-3681-5

ISBN 13 Large Print: 978-0-7684-3682-2

ISBN 13 Ebook: 978-0-7684-9027-5

For Worldwide Distribution, Printed in the U.S.A.

1 2 3 4 5 6 7 8 9 10 11 / 13 12 11 10

Dedication

In loving and adoring memory of my father, Todd W. Orr, and to countless children around the globe who have awakened me to love and be loved—who have all shared with me in coming face to face with Jesus in the dirt.

Acknowledgments

To my husband, Joshua, for his undying love and courage to run after the outrageous heartbeat of God for our lives.

To my parents, Greg and Jody Mootz, for giving me a place away to write, think, and dream, and for their constant encouragement to keep going on an unpaved road.

To my Papaw, Bob Stanforth, whose stories make me laugh, for being my biggest fan and teaching me about life and what is to come. To the rest of my family for their distinct role in making me who I have become.

To Bob and Gracie Ekblad, for their constant prayers and encouragement, and for sticking with me through the good times and the bad. Thanks for letting me be a part of your journey.

To Leilani Rector, for all her prayers, encouragement, and amazing editing skills.

To Rolland and Heidi Baker, for all of their support, and for their life example that has kept me running after "Jesus in the dirt."

To Michele Perry, for her unyielding friendship, inspiration, and giggles along the dirt roads of Africa's heart.

To Randi Blick, for being my best friend, and for taking the risk and launching out onto an unpaved road. For her constant upbeat spirit and love that could shake nations.

To Nate Blick, for joining us in Africa and, along the way, creating memories that make us buckle with laughter-filled tears. For his comedic spirit that always kept our hearts ready for more along the journey's way.

To Nathan Scott, for his initial prophetic word so many years ago that this book would come to life, and for being such a great mentor, even an ocean away.

To Alyn and A.J. Jones, for being a part of my story and for inviting me into their family.

To the Holy Given and Iris family—you know who you are. Keep running to the ends of the earth.

To the children of Africa who have kept me in constant amazement at the mystery of encountering love face to face in the world around me.

Endorsements

Only people who have been desert-trained can be true prophets. Only people who have been broken can bring outrageous healing and wholeness. Those who know hiddenness with God get to revel in Manifest Presence. When you can truly dwell amongst the poorest, you can be trusted with Heaven's riches. Those who suffer at the hands of a sin-sick world can take captivity captive. To become the friends of God, we must learn obedience as humble servants.

Can you see the pattern of God's dealings? This is not a "made for television" spiritual life where everything turns out right between the last set of commercials and the credits. Our passion for God and our compassion for people are tested continuously so that our identity develops to the same height as the Father's intentionality. What would it take for you to believe that God is unceasingly magnificent to you always, even in the midst of personal pain and tragedy?

Jess knows the kiss of God. She has been to hell and prospered. She knows the heights and the depths of God's love. If you are fortunate enough to be called to an outrageous life of fellowship with God, then this is your manual, your journal, and the outline to your story. Only the brave will read it!

Graham Cooke
Author and speaker
www.grahamcooke.com

There is much being written on the love of God these days, and rightly so—it is the desperately needed message of the hour. Jessica's book is the gripping story of what happens to a human heart once it has been seized by the radical love of God. It will inspire you to lay hold of the Great Commandment and then the Great Commission, so that you, too, will become a laid-down lover for the Kingdom of God.

John Arnott
Founding pastor, TACF and Catch the Fire Ministries
www.tacf.org, www.johnandcarol.org

What an incredible book! *For Love's Sake* will teach you how to love with actions way beyond words. There is a depth of love that can only be found by walking through wickedness and hatred, a love that produces freedom only through ultimate surrender. You will be challenged and changed by Jessica's story of learning to love.

Wesley and Stacey Campbell
RevivalNOW Ministries
Board members, Iris Ministries
Be a Hero
www.beahero.org

To truly know love is to be love. Jessica is one who has embraced a lifestyle of the heart of Jesus. She is taking the message of loving the widowed, the orphaned, and the poor out of the four walls of the church. She is a voice calling out, "Come, join the laid-down lovers of Jesus Christ."

For Love's Sake is not a book for the satisfied; this is a radical look into the sometimes brutal reality of life without hope. Jessica shares her stories across the globe as she is "compelled by the gaze of love." She writes the "chronicles of the nobodies" in the hopes that the reader, too, will be captivated by God's heart and say yes to making a difference. There are great joys and unimaginable heartaches, and yet triumph prevails. I invite you to join the author on this journey of a lifetime.

Randy Clark
President, Apostolic Network of Global Awakening
Mechanicsburg, Pennsylvania
www.globalawakening.com

Listen to a totally surrendered life that captures the attention of Heaven. Open your ears to hear the call of God for the poor of the earth. Step into the journey of abandonment through the prophetic story of Mary, the mother of Jesus, together with Jess's raw missionary experiences. This book will grip your heart for the poor and impart God's heart cry to you!

Ché Ahn
Senior pastor, Harvest Rock Church
President and founder, Harvest International Ministry
www.harvestrockchurch.org

Jessica's book, *For Love's Sake*, carries the heartbeat of one who hungered for faith and found it, one who longed for fulfilled destiny and discovered it, one who longed to fulfill the dream that God had placed in her and is living it! I was moved by the emphasis that Jessica placed on the relationship between cost and love, suffering and joy. It is evident that the maturity God has grown in Jessica releases something that we all need to hear and makes this book worthy of reading. I truly am looking forward to hearing of the impact this book will have on many lives—those looking to fulfill the dreams they have, too!

Danny Steyne
Mountain of Worship
www.mountainofworship.org

The journey that Jessica Davis bids us—dares us—to join is a journey with Jesus and "the least of these," who, in the upside-down Kingdom, turn out to be the teachers of those who have ears to hear. Jessica has provided supportive encouragement to us by recounting her own story of God's miraculous hand in her journeys around the world. *For Love's Sake* is also worth the read just for the imaginative and powerful way Jessica has interwoven the story of Mary, the mother of Jesus, throughout her own narrative. Allowing God to overshadow us, as Mary did, is the vital key to *receiving* and living the Kingdom journey.

Dr. John Hurtgen
Dean, School of Theology, Campbellsville University
Campbellsville, Kentucky
www.campbellsville.edu

Virgil, one of Rome's greatest poets, said, "Love conquers all." The Beatles said, "All you need is love." The ancient Greeks made a practice of analyzing love until it was almost beyond recognition. Shamans, poets, philosophers, preachers, rabbis, and sages have endeavored to define this mystery for the rest of us. However, when the music is over and the dancing has stopped, when words are powerless and voices of reason are silent, God watches for opportunities to awaken that indescribable force in us. God, who is Love, has given Jessica a special grace to remind us all that demonstrations are more powerful than definitions, and that, in the end, love never fails.

Ray Hughes
Selah Ministries
www.selahministries.com

Contents

Foreword

by Rolland & Heidi Baker

For Love's Sake is a book that I would recommend all our missionaries and missions school students to read. It's not just creatively and beautifully written. It's not just appealing to the adventurous and young at heart. It doesn't just have amazing miracle stories or engaging tales of travel, exploration, and discovery. It's not just extravagant, daring, wild, and crazy and filled with lessons in cross-cultural awareness and sensitivity. It's not even just an appeal to remember the poor.

It is all these things, but more importantly it is an inspired reversal of common perceptions of the Kingdom that do violence to the plainest teachings of Scripture. It gives breathtaking hope to the hungriest of the hungry and the most desperate of all who refuse any substitutes for the full force of God's Presence. Jessica Davis was driven away from Christianity as she knew it in the West, and she was willing to search the earth to find her heart's desire. *For Love's Sake* is a record of what she found.

Jessica's book is a window into the core values of Iris Ministries, which we believe are simply ordinary and should be normal for ministries everywhere. Jesus ought to be the primary attraction of the Christian life, and to find and know Him should be a goal that towers above all others. But Jessica has come to understand something. Jesus is the image of the invisible God, and His life perfectly reflects the values of an upside-down Kingdom in our midst.

The Messiah was expected to dominate, take over, impress with His power and superiority in every earthly realm. He could have brought the glories of Heaven to earth in a dazzling way, overcoming all opposition with His super-natural Presence and legions of angels. His disciples were frustrated and impatient, wondering when He would exert Himself as they thought He should.

Instead, He presented Himself as the Good Shepherd, giving His life for His sheep. He modeled a gentleness and lowliness that belied His power and authority. With compassion He responded to the meek and poor, leaving the arrogant and self-sufficient to their own devices. He knew His own value, and in perfect love He explained that those who were not prepared to give up all that they had for His sake were not worthy of Him.

Our chief value in Iris Ministries is to find God in the face of Christ, not placing any of our own limits on the degree to which we can actually know and experience Him. God promises His people, *"You will seek Me and find Me, when you search for Me with all your heart"* (Jer. 29:13 NKJV). What does it mean to actually find Him? More than we ever dreamed!

The question then becomes, where do we look for Him? Where is a likely place for revival? What does God value, and what does God reward? Heidi and I came to the poorest nation we could find in large part as a response to my grandfather's missionary example in China. Instead of starting at the top with those most "likely" to be of influence, leaders of state, church, and business, he started at the bottom with "the least of these." He and my grand-mother took in starving, dying beggar children, and other missionaries criti-cized him for wasting his time. But God knew how to glorify Himself by displaying His matchless grace. He poured out His Spirit on these ignorant, helpless children, bringing conviction, revelation, and gifting in His Presence to a degree unheard of in Church history. Truly He showed Himself to be an upside-down God, caring where nobody else cared, redeeming the useless and hopeless, transforming the ungrateful and unworthy. He chooses the weak and lowly things of this world to nullify the great, so that no one can be proud before Him.

So Heidi and I learned to look for Jesus in the faces of the poor, and to anticipate revival and the Presence of God on the low rungs of the ladder of society and culture. Jessica has learned the same thing from her spiritual and geographical treks to the poor, the underside of the earth. God can bring revival anywhere, and He has given us increased compassion for the poor in spirit wherever they are, but the cry of our hearts is to go lower still and find God where He is most likely to be found, at the bottom.

We are in Mozambique to see a continuation of the revival my grandfather witnessed, and now, after 15 years here, we are seeing a people movement that is changing the nation. We came with the simple intention of taking in a few orphans, but Jesus responded by pouring out His fiery love, fueling a wildfire that has leapfrogged from village to village in the bush until thousands of churches have been birthed in all ten provinces.

Heidi and I are encouraged to read in Jessica's book that one of her first intense experiences of encountering the Presence of God was under our green-and-white striped tent at our main base in Pemba. In the dirt with wind and dust blowing, dripping in the heat, and holy chaos all around, Jessica found what she had not been able to receive on thick carpets, in air-conditioned sanctuaries, and from polished programs. She found that Jesus was willing to show Himself to her in a most unlikely environment in an insignificant little town in the remote bush of one of the poorest and most unknown countries in the world.

And Jessica encountered power, the power of our perfect Savior and Almighty God. Not only do we need to find God personally and value His Presence above everything, but we also must utterly depend on His power to sustain us miraculously in all things. From support to food to healing and every kind of blessing, we look to God for what we need and want. *For Love's Sake* is an epic of Jessica's experience in learning to trust God, just as the poor must. Without the power of God, we run up against our limits immediately in facing the vast need of most of the world. We share Jessica's excitement in refusing to put our own limits on what we can ask of Jesus, and her exhilaration at finding herself able to exercise faith that is so graciously and increasingly poured out on the humble and childlike.

Jessica also learned with us that the cup Jesus has asked us to drink is the same one that He drank, a cup of both suffering and joy. We will share in Jesus' glory forever provided that we also share in His sufferings. There is a perfect reason for this. We counter the idea that Jesus suffered so that we would never have to. But suffering according to the will of God has value, and it is a necessary component of the Christian life. It corrects us, proves the genuineness of our faith, and keeps us humble and dependent on God who raises the dead. When we are weak, we are strong, so we delight in our weaknesses that the power of God may rest on us.

But suffering is not the end of the story. Through many tribulations we enter the Kingdom of God, but He delivers us out of them all! We aim for the outcome of God's dealings with us, and the joy with which we are rewarded for living life amid evil opposition by participating in the divine nature of Jesus Himself. No amount of temporary earthly blessing could ever replace hearing the words, *"Well done, good and faithful servant! You have been faithful with a few things; I will put you in charge of many things. Come and share your master's happiness!"* (Matt. 25:23 NIV).

Jessica chronicles her sufferings as well, sometimes intense. Finding our way to Jesus and eternal life may cost us everything. We must choose between this life and the next, and there is no middle ground. Jessica became a laid-down lover of Jesus. She has received the priceless gift of hunger, and is reaping her reward. I know this book will bring many along the same road she has journeyed, different in particulars, but identical in spirit. May their encounters with Jesus surpass all expectations!

Rolland & Heidi Baker
Directors, Iris Ministries
Pemba, Mozambique
July 2010

Chapter 1

In Heaven's Shadow

"To live would be an awfully big adventure." —Peter Pan

I am caught in a beautiful and blinding morning. The world outside begins to breathe, and sounds of life stir around me. Outside my window—which is really a hole in a feeble dirt wall—I can hear the giggles of children as they run barefoot through the dust. They are so close to the mud wall separating us that I can hear their breath as they wait for me to emerge from my room. I am alive. More so than I have ever known in my life.

The hot sun of Africa is hovering over us with little mercy, but under its radiance, somehow life makes sense. At 120 degrees Fahrenheit the sun can bring life or death. In this moment, my spirit chooses to receive life. I leave the solidarity of my room and am instantly transported to another realm—my "God in a box" mind-set is reduced to ashes. Tiny, dirt-covered hands are reaching for mine, and early morning embraces are full of more energy than I can muster. With eyes closed and my face turned upward toward Heaven, I feel the missing pieces finally snap into place. The puzzle of my heart comes into alignment with Heaven's rhythm, and this time its cadence feels like my own. Somehow, every little finger attached to every child around me finds real estate on my arms and legs, and all manage to cling to the hem of my skirt—which is dragging in the dirt beneath us. In this inside-out Kingdom, there's always enough. And in this moment, I am awakened—soul deep.

In this place there are times that I still pinch myself to figure out if I am dreaming or awake. Looking down at my dirt-covered feet in a pair of sandals that have traveled over 100,000 miles, the realization unfolds—I am home. And this home is not a geographical address, but a spiritual navigation. It's the Heaven on earth we've all been created for.

How do you find a hidden homeland that has all too often been forgotten? How did I get here? That is the question I ask myself every day. I got here through an uncommon door—the heart of Jesus. His heart beats a message that shows us the way to go. I followed children and the poor around the world through a low door. The road maps I had been given along the way simply got me nowhere. In the end, I didn't need directions. What I needed was a willingness to go anywhere to find it.

Have you ever been so close to the face of another that you can feel his heartbeat? I looked into Jesus' eyes of fiery love one day and was forever marked by His gaze. What does it feel like to be face to face with Jesus? I liken it to the fashioning of a diamond. A little piece of coal, black and dull, is placed before a force that consumes its very being. What is left after its encounter? Radiant beauty—enough to make the whole world look on in wonder of such a creation. The relationship between the two is outrageous and upside down. But the results rouse the curiosity of all who look on.

Herein enters the upturned trade that takes place. We give ourselves to God—masked by debris from our lives of pain, hopelessness, and need—and the impact of just being near who He is uncovers who we have been designed to be from beneath the carnage of who we believed we were. There's not a five-point plan to get there—no secret and expensive formula to buy. Somehow, we've been sold an idea of Jesus that is synonymous with cartoon-like myths like the Easter Bunny, the Tooth Fairy, and Santa Claus. And sometimes when we see Him for who He really is, He doesn't look at all as we had imagined or thought. Regardless of what it looks like for each of us to meet with God, this imprinting exchange is still made.

It was in the depths of His heart that I learned about love. I was expecting a fairy tale-like adventure where everything ends "happily ever after." But what I found was a love that gives itself for its enemy. There are no guarantees that the one who loves won't get bruised of heart or spirit. Following the path of most convenience leads us nowhere in the same way that buying a cheap card leads us to romance. It's not a love that is pasted on Valentine endeavors, but its cost goes much deeper than our wallets. How many of us have been taught how to budget for love? Are we willing to commit to the investment?

Heaven's clock is different. We give God our lives, but our lives are a stream of todays. What starts out as a small "yes" for today—a commitment despite the inconvenience that it brings—develops into a life-long roller coaster-like ride of raw faith that is filled with many ups and downs along the way. A lifetime of experiences in that place seems like only a moment here.

One glance into those deep eyes awakens us to find the place we have been created for. You know something else about those eyes that have captured me? Each time Jesus shows me His face I see the marriage of some of the most opposite things. In His eyes, I have seen hunger and fullness together. I have seen suffering and joy—all in the radiance of one glance.

Through the Back Door

I sat down one day to write about a journey around the world. One where my only possessions were loosely tossed into a backpack, and my teachers were hidden behind the guise of children's faces. The word *pilgrimage* comes from the Latin word *peregrinus*, which means "a person wandering the earth in exile, someone in search of a spiritual homeland."[1] That is me in a nutshell. And those wanderings are what make my life worthwhile.

Why did I want to write this story? On my journey around the world, I would learn volumes of lessons through chance encounters with others who taught me the beginning of learning to love. These stories connect you to more than the life of an ordinary young woman like me, but can link you to the untold existence of those who turned my world inside out. The memoirs of the broken ones echo throughout the earth. *Their* story is *our* story. It may be in vogue to know *your* life and embrace *your* reality and *your* purpose, but I set out to know *our* story—the chronicles of the nobodies with a shared heart and need. A family dynasty, if you will. What is this shared crux? It is an imprinting of DNA within us that draws us to discovering our true identity. It is a place where we uncover Heaven's reflection in the eyes of one another side by side.

I am hoping to reveal a glance through the windowpane of Heaven, from Heaven's perspective. That glimpse is a call to a place of abandon, generated from encounters with another realm. That's a part of the tale. What's more, I wanted to strip "living with the poor" down to its raw, naked reality. Jesus didn't just "work" with the poor. He decided to come as one of them, live alongside of them, sit next to them, and struggle with them through the realities of life.

Whether we know it or not, we are all somewhat spiritually bankrupt—poor in spirit. We've invested our livelihoods into so many "pyramid scams" in life and faith. We've bought into an idea of a Jesus that is marketed to us—you and I—with bonus accessories to "dress" Him up to our liking—to match ourselves. We've bought and invested into a lie.

Jesus threw His life away for Love. His craving is simply for us to do the same. What does it mean to "give your life away" for Love—Himself? I was often swept up in the romanticism of missions—an outrageous relationship with God—and working in the most desolate places on the earth. The Hollywood-meets-Disney production of a life lived in that manner captivated me. Miracles are real, and you'll get plenty of that reality within these few pages. There is, however, another side. What I call the *underside*. People most often give odes to the *good* that comes with being on the mission field—the glitz, the grandeur, and the glamour of it all. What about the bad, the ugly, and the sometimes tragic face of laying your life down? Pain, suffering, hunger, and disappointment can hit you with what feels like a greater force at times than witnessing a blind man see before your eyes.

The underside starts at the bottom and works its way up. It begins in a state of emptiness. And in the dust is where I am inviting you to join me on this journey. What does it mean to follow Jesus in the dirt? Could it possibly be an invitation to suffering, too? Could it be more than giggles and gumdrops? The world that I live in encompasses both of these realities. The coexistence of Heaven and hell, suffering and joy, love and hate. The tug-of-war that operates within the opposite functions of reward and cost, laughter and weeping, even giving and receiving—all of these movements in one instant. What do we do in the fog that remains? What is our response? This book opens the entryway in thinking through and wrestling with these hard questions aloud.

Here's your chance. Throw your backpack on your shoulder and step in with me on this backward path. Some of us have become used to going through the "right" door—the one located out front leading to a ladder climb that "commercialized" faith and modern politics have set up as a standard before us. I am inviting you through the back door of a life laid down for Love. Are we willing to join the poor, the sick, the needy, and the childlike in this search for what quenches our thirst? Jesus is looking for those who will make their home in Him and follow Him wherever He goes. He saves us a seat on the margins to fuse our hearts with His. A low road is opened up for us to choose to step onto, where we come upon a hub outside the borders. It is a place where, together, we sit and watch Him erect palaces in the dust—a Kingdom in our midst.

This is not a journey for the faint of heart. It is a trek to the underside, from the bottom up, where Jesus shows us what life can look like with the offering up of our lives to God, extreme need, and all of Heaven behind us. The way of Jesus in all its messiness and beauty.

Jesus didn't become famous on earth as a rich man who "saved" the poor using His dominion and might. No one expected the King set to inherit Israel to come as a slave. It was not only unheard of, but also patently offensive to Israelis awaiting their conquering Supremo! But this Rogue's outright strategy seems to be the element of surprise. Upside down is just His nature. The wildest part of it all is that He asks us to join in with Him and other nobodies to see what can happen on the outskirts of society when a few outcasts say "yes" to envisioning a world where what *is* transforms into a new reality. This is an untamed road meant for us to trek together. What could happen if we began to search for this place alongside one another? What steps do we need to take in order to get there? What would you say if I told you it was as easy as saying "yes" to the plans of God for your life—your own distinct journey of learning to love?

Laid-down living doesn't have to be complicated. Love is simple. What we will realize is that Heaven will become our classroom. Life hasn't always looked this way at all. With only a whisper, the winds changed and I found myself in a land that transformed the way I would see the world forever.

Lives Interrupted by Heaven's Touch

I didn't find Jesus in books or even in classrooms of theological training centers. Trust me, I tried! Sure, I attempted to go through the conventional entrances, the right doors. I took a stab at climbing the "ladder" put before me and strove with all my might to jump through the constant array of political "hoops." I just had no luck! I found Jesus in the most unlikely of places—in the lowly huddling in the dirt. It was in the eyes of the children and the poor that I was able to stare into His face here on the earth.

The morning after my high school graduation, I got on a plane headed to Africa. Why? That's the question I get the most even to this day. I wasn't quite sure. All I knew was that I heard Jesus whisper, "Go." I am the type of girl who, when Jesus says to jump, I don't even ask how high, I just jump with all of my might. And the next thing I knew, I was on the ground enveloped in the countless sounds, sights, and smells of that beautiful land. It was like I was experiencing an expanded spiritual dimension. I felt like the Grinch on Christmas when his heart grew two sizes!

I used to think that missions—or living a radical life for God in the earth—consisted of loud-mouthed, sunburned Westerners shouting "amens" from a wooden platform. Now I know it is attained in lowliness—an act of "downward mobility"[2] where we intentionally choose a low road that goes completely against the seat of dominance and eminence we've been born into. Only then can we receive the nations as our inheritance (see Ps. 2:8 NIV). I thought it was about bringing Jesus into the entire world. Little did I know that He was already there when my plane landed!

Perhaps you picked up this book because you thought it was about supernatural living or mission work, or about adventures into the unknowns of Africa and beyond. And in part, it is. But the real substance of this story is discovered within an overshadowing from Heaven. That is the true story—a life interrupted by Heaven's touch.

A Life Overshadowed

Let me jump-start our journey by inviting you into the lives of two mismatched young women from different centuries with surprising similarities: Mary—the mother of Jesus—and none other than yours truly. Each of our stories catches us in humble settings, surprised by God's invitation to take us on a journey into faith to behold Jesus—lives interrupted by Heaven's touch. Let's rewind to Mary's day and take a sneak peek into her first break-in from Heaven.

The night was similar to any other night. The quietness was in stark contrast to the daytime hustle and bustle of a long day's work. Yet in the stillness, her heart pounded with anticipation. Why? She had no idea. Still, as her body nearly drifted off to sleep, Mary's heart remained awake. She was young and the busyness of wedding preparations was clouding her mind.

There was so much to be done and so little time. As she lay in bed, her mind raced, tracing the list of items to be checked off for the "big day." Did she finish the list? What was left unfinished? Was the temple ready? Were all the guests coming? Would she be ready in time?

In the stillness of the night, her life suddenly took a drastic change. A messenger was in front of her whose image emanated light that nearly blinded her eyes. What could this be? The motion beside her caught her attention. Her hands were trembling from surprise. Whatever was happening was not normal in her everyday life experience.

"You are highly favored, Mary," he said. Her very being shook with bewilderment. Who was this man now standing in front of her? She wanted to run, but there was nowhere to go. And the more she lingered, the more she felt magnetized to stay. Her mind again raced with possible answers, but still she was left empty.

What came next would send her into a journey that no one on earth could have led her on. She was a teenager, and the messenger simply said, "Mary, God loves you, and He has chosen you to carry His Son. He is going to be a king, the King of kings in fact, and His Kingdom will never end."

The angel left only step one of her directions—name Him Jesus.

"How could this be?" she asked. She was no different from anyone else. Had she been searching or asking for this break-in? She was simply minding her own business in her everyday life. How could she possibly carry Heaven? It was too much, wasn't it? It was an impossible question. Yet, the messenger did not ask her. He only let her know what would be.

It wouldn't be wise. What would people think? She was not even married! What would her family say? What would the temple crowd remark? Do you even know what happens to women who find themselves pregnant out of wedlock? All of these questions ran through her mind.

She could be stoned to death. How would she explain herself? This had never been done before in history, had it? Who would believe her testimony? Think of the reproach!

Then it suddenly dawned on her—what would Joseph think? Would he even believe her? Was she hallucinating? She checked her pulse just to make sure. Would this ruin her life plans?

Yet the look in his eyes captivated her.

"Heaven will overshadow you, Mary," he said. "Nothing is impossible with God."

"All you have to do is say 'yes.' Heaven will do the rest."

Questions continued to flood her mind. She was young but she wasn't stupid. "Do you know what this means?" a voice asked her.

But…his eyes. She could feel the immense presence of Heaven upon her already. A minute seemed as if it was longer than eternity as questions and fears enveloped her. In spite of that, she felt more alive in this moment than she could ever remember. Standing there, she stood face to face with her future. A mirror image of her destiny resonated in front of her eyes in the messenger's stare.

The only words that she could muster were, "Let it be to me as you have said." All she could whisper was, "Yes."

That "yes" would cost her everything.

Without as much as a good-bye the visitor was gone, and Mary was left wondering about this visitation. What now? What did this overshadowing mean?

In the months that followed, Mary began to see, feel, and live out the effects of such an encounter. Soon, she could feel the pulsating rhythm of Heaven within her. She carried the heartbeat of Heaven. One overshadowing from Heaven changed the entire world. And it was ushered in by a small whisper of, "Yes."

What was Mary's cry? "Let it be to me as you have said."

It is a heart cry of a life given away for Love. Mary's cry is our heart's cry.

Just One Look

One connection with Heaven changed Mary's entire life direction. The everyday was invaded with eternity, and nothing in her life was left untouched. We are all invited to collide with Heaven. Mary was minding her own business and ended up meeting with God. The aftermath of that encounter opened a door for all of us to enter into a lifestyle of meeting with Heaven and partnering with God in His heart for the world around us. One meeting with God—one connection with Heaven—changed the earth forever.

It is true that I hopped on an airplane to a very foreign land at a young age. I had one goal in mind—to meet with God. But to be honest with you, I had no idea what that would look like. And the way in which I would crash into a real-life encounter of my own was definitely not what I had been asking for—or expecting, for that matter!

In an instant, all that I had known as reality moments before seemed the most distant memory I possessed. Everything that had been around me was now unseen and the very unseen things were more real than I had ever imagined. Colors seemed more radiant than one could express or explain, and in a flash, I found my heart at rest.

That didn't stop the pounding of my heartbeat from increasing, however. This place I was now in was the most familiar yet foreign location that I have ever experienced. One meeting with Jesus would shake my entire being. The odd part was, I was home. This was the place I was created for.

His eyes were more gripping than the force of gravity. The pull that they exerted bonded my gaze to His. Still, each time I looked, I felt as if I would be consumed at any moment. One minute, I was immersed in my normal everyday life. The next, I was in another realm that I had little idea even existed.

Soaring temperatures blanketed Africa's famous red dust. I was worshiping in the rich dirt underneath a large white-and-green-striped tent one afternoon in the blistering heat. Somehow, whenever we worshiped, the wind came. Enough wind to blow your hair back from your face in one refreshing swoop. I can remember little black and brown hands clinging to my skirt and adoration for Jesus filling the air. Sound like a fairy tale? Most truly real things do.

The place I was now in was seamless—there was no beginning and no end. The sights and sounds I had known only a breath before were a distant memory, and all that I could focus on now was the reality of what was before me—or rather, *Who* was.

The look in Jesus' eyes made me want to hide because of its intensity, but at the same time, His eyes locked mine in their gaze. This was what Heaven was like. What else was happening? I don't really know. All I could attend to was those eyes.

Every color possible encompassed them. I saw the fullness of emotion openly expressed in them. It was as if His eyes told the story. And you know what? As much wonder as I had for Jesus, I noticed He had the same for me. It was a look of amazement and intrigue that He carried. His face showed wonder and fascination as He was present with me.

He knew me completely. I was transparent, and while looking at Jesus, I was learning things about who I *really* was. I was in a state of identity realized.

Meeting with Heaven wasn't at all like I had imagined. It wasn't a quiet place with clean walls and organization. It was holy chaos! Worship was moving and loud. This place was alive and breathing. Colors engulfed the air, which blew freely around the place. Life was breathing, not stagnant, here.

How did I get here? His hunger drew me. I think it was a constant beckoning where Jesus would find ways in my life to draw me closer to Himself in times that transcended the thickness of time or space. All I knew was that in this place I was free, and it was where I wanted to live and never leave.

Jesus took my hand in His. I was trying to get my bearings in the midst of the power that flowed from Him. I was caught up in this whirlwind that filled me with so much love that I thought I could not contain myself for a second longer.

This location was where I was meant to live.

Echoes in Eternity

I watched as Jesus poured oil and wine over my hand. *What was He asking?* I thought. Then He asked me, "Will you go with Me to the place I want to show you?"

I heard their footsteps before I saw their faces.

I had walked straight into an encounter I had not planned on or asked for. The voices of children filled the air. It was thick with laughter and cries, a complexity of both of these.

And then, there He was. My Jesus. Encircled by multitudes of children of every color. There were yellow ones, black ones, brown ones, and white ones. Each child resembled Him, and they carried His image.

I was overwhelmed by the weight of the stares of thousands of little ones beckoning me with their countenance. The air around us was heavy and swirling. Each child was moving toward me, reaching for my grasp.

Then I recognized them—finally understanding where they had come from.

The crowd that was in front of me were children around the world exploited by war, disease, and death. They were the fatherless hidden around the globe. They each had a name, each had a story, and all were looking straight into my eyes.

They were crying out, "Mama!" and all I could do was weep at the weight of their declaration. In this place I felt weaker than I can express. My eyes widened in wonder, extreme shock, and utter dismay. What was I to do with thousands of children?

How could I be a mother? I was just a young girl myself! Hearing the questions racing through my mind, Jesus looked into my eyes and said, "As I rescued you, rescue them. I died to purchase their freedom, and they belong to Me!"

What did that mean? I didn't understand. That moment in time lasted for what seemed like forever. The echoes of those words of His still flow in waves over my memory. Heaven had visited me. What was I supposed to do now?

And just as quickly as He had come, Jesus was gone. That was it. I was left face first in the African dirt for what seemed like eternity trying to recover from what I had just encountered. I was shaking under the weight of His words.

The children I had grown to love already were gathered around me, watching and waiting for a sign of life. They knew where I had been. They would teach me more about the place I had just been than I knew. They, too, had each made their home there. Each had met with God and their lives were changed because of it.

Why do I do what I do? I live my life in this way because Jesus asked me to. I was ruined for anything else a long time ago. It didn't take me long to decide; one look into those eyes of His and all I could cry was, "Yes!" There was no looking back. The aftermath of that meeting launched my life into a completely different direction than I had ever expected.

Treasures Along the Roadside

Since that fateful day in Africa, my journey has been a constant collision of two realms. An expedition where we—the team I have gained along the way and myself—have lost ourselves in the reality of Heaven crashing into the earth. The impact that most always results from a face-to-face run-in with the unmasked reflection of who we really are at our core. The good, the bad, and the ugly come to bat on the same playing field. Call it the beginning of learning how to love.

Along the way, I discovered jewels hidden within the earth. Gems that taught me more than any formal training could disclose. They each have names and carry stories of their own. Many are written about within these pages.

When I began this search on an unpaved road of nearly two dozen countries, I am not sure I knew what I was looking for. Somehow, in the midst of some of the most obscure locations on the planet, I found Him. The One my heart loves.

I can remember sitting in the African dirt one morning in a village named Magugu. I was the only foreigner there at the time, and Khadija, a four-year-old, was sitting with me. Soon, without advertisement, a dozen more children were surrounding us. Without hesitation, I quickly became the neighborhood "couch." As giggles and laughter filled the air, time for me nearly stood still. I was capturing a glimpse of perfection, a place where Heaven and earth dance together in one accord. I was beginning to see with new eyes. My teachers? They were all under the age of five.

We are all on this pilgrimage. It is a quest of learning to see with new eyes the world around us. Perhaps these are ramblings of eclectic musings around the globe. Really, they are the stammering for words to describe what it is like to see light encapsulate the darkness and a divine Kingdom in the dust. This is our shared trek together—a trip to the low place of love—and all the stops and memories along the way. It is the story of the "climb" that we each undergo in searching for a supernatural existence.

Face to Face With Love

Have you ever seen your reflection in the eyes of another? It is as if you have seen yourself for the first time for who you truly are and who he or she sees you to be.

I was 13 years old when the presence of Jesus came and visited me for four nights at 1:04 in the morning. Sound crazy? It should. I was completely shocked and, honestly, freaked out! This most certainly was not part of the Sunday school lessons of the past that I had filed into my memory. My only grid was in gluing cotton balls on paper sheep and cookies with punch. No one ever told me about Jesus showing up in my room!

In a not-so-soft whisper, I heard Jesus say, "You will be a missionary and a minister. Remember, always run to Me." Each night He would whisper these words to me, and each time I wondered how this would translate into my everyday life. Love had walked into my room. When He left, my only reaction was to run after Him and follow Him wherever He went in the best way I knew how.

Groggy under the stupor of sleep deprivation that week, my head was in the clouds. What did He mean? How would this change my life? And how was I supposed to return to my ordinary everyday life?

The aftermath of this visitation was a whirlwind of places and times spent on my face, drawn away to a place only with Him. The rest is history. I was caught up in His gaze, and along the way, He would help me stay there when I didn't have the muscle to remain.

Whispers of Promise

Walking down the dirt road one day, the village kids around me were more numerous than usual, and I had about 20 vying for my two hands. Encircled within them, I could hear "Mama Jessica" being shouted as they were struggling for a spot closest within my reach. These are the times when my heart leaps from within my chest—when the dirt becomes like Heaven—and their little faces become forever engrained in my memory.

As their cries of "Mama Jessica" echo through the air, I can hear the whispers of Heaven, and I remember the encounters that changed me forever.

More than the supernatural piece of an outrageous life with Jesus, the times of holding children in my arms around the world have shaped who I am. They have taught me how to be a daughter by being a student eagerly learning from such childlike wisdom beyond their years. Maybe children just innately understand the mysteries of the Kingdom of Heaven. I am beginning to believe it.

A Hidden Kingdom

Jumping on an airplane, I traveled to Mexico at the age of 15. I came because I wanted to see. I needed to really become immersed in the reality of life beyond my own backyard. Not just to experience the reality of human poverty. I wanted more than just being a spectator in my own life.

The smell of the garbage dump flooded my sinuses. The early morning air was dry and full of the stench of burning rubbish. I had followed Love into the middle of a dump in Tijuana, Mexico. The narrow streets of the city were crowded with people. Morning was in full swing.

The view from the top startled me. Shanties were the very structures holding up this massive landfill. My first reaction was that of pity. "Why?" was my attempt at forming words for what I was encountering. "We have to do something," was my attempt at action.

Then I heard Him say, "Look again."

As I looked I saw them—countless children running toward me, all giggling and cooing words of *hola*. I was their object of study for the day. I can still feel the warm air circling around me. I can still feel their tiny hands clinging to mine.

I was beginning to see. There was a hidden Kingdom in the ashes of that burning garbage. I was beginning to catch a view underneath what I thought was—to a different reality—and catching the rhythm of Heaven. Heaven on earth looked so much different than I had expected. This day, I was learning to see as Jesus saw. Revival could look so very upside down to what I had imagined. Here, I had captured it in one look in a child's eyes.

South of the Border

Lalo and Oscar were my favorite little boys at the children's center that I worked in. Can we have favorites? I think so. In any case, they are the ones that forever hold a place in my heart.

They were brothers. Both of these young ones were smaller than four feet tall and under the age of seven. Lalo reminded me of Ricky Ricardo and carried the same nature of comedy in his spirit. Oscar was gentle and sweet and gave the best hugs south of the border. They were my first instructors in this upside-down Kingdom that I was chasing after.

Lalo would sneak up on me to surprise me with his usual spunk during the oddest parts of the day. I can remember one afternoon when he burst into the room and began singing at the top of his little lungs. What's more, he had a suit on for a coming *quinceanera* party—a traditional Mexican celebration to honor a young girl turning 15 and becoming a woman. So picture a three-foot little ball of comedy with a cheeky, unforgettable grin and voice that could hit the rafters, flinging the door wide open to put on a show—just for you. It instantly triggered a memory of an episode of *I Love Lucy*. I was erupting with laughter-filled tears.

Maybe that is the point of these years of learning. Perhaps these moments are what we have been created for—these times when Heaven will burst in unannounced just to simply be with us. The simple dirt paths of Mexico became the first steps on the yellow brick road to my proverbial Land of Oz. And along the way, I would meet many who were on a similar pilgrimage to this land of desire.

Heaven's Hunger

On this lifelong trip I have looked into the eyes of children and seen Jesus staring back at me. It wrecked me forever. They are my greatest teachers and have given me childlike hope—a belief that says that no matter how much devastation exists around us, Heaven's help can change everything. In them I have captured what it is like to walk hand in hand with Jesus into the dark and see Him love as He loves. They have given me eyes to see Heaven regained and the dance that can happen when I place my tiny feet on the shoes of a big God who shows me what to do each step of the way. They've given me a gift of dependence, one that I will carry with me forever.

After nearly two years from the first time I stepped foot in Africa, I set out through Africa and the Middle East because of a whisper from God one night under the stars in Mozambique. Looking back it makes me laugh. When I close my eyes I can see it all again. All the places, the people, the sights, the smells begin to come to life once more. I am there again. I have gained more than memories. I have received a family.

This journey is for the hungry because it is about the hungry. It is about what can happen when the hungry go after that which their souls long for. Two things can happen to a hungry man—he can starve or he can eat. This, too, is our choice. A place where hunger is married to fullness is where we can now reside.

Created for Encounter

As you glance at the pictures of children from the farthest places of the earth—in television commercials, magazine exposés, and other globetrotting adventures—what do you see?

Look again. Can you see it? There is a kingdom and literal palaces in the mud. That is what I see. I can look at a slum and see royalty. It is as if we roll the red carpet out as Jesus steps barefoot into the reality of human suffering. With new eyes, we can see what truly is. Where Heaven is, everything transforms by a single touch.

Do you know what else? It has a way of drawing you into that realm. This is what we have been created for—encounters with Heaven that remind us of our true home, one that many of us have forgotten somehow.

Go ahead and let yourself be pulled into this place of encounter. Come meet with God wherever you find yourself. It is the place you were fashioned for. This is not a story of an unusual life. It is an invitation to be wooed into the shadow of Jesus.

This, too, is for you.

For Love's Sake

Why does God desire to visit each of us in our ordinary lives? Mary was a young village girl in Nazareth who was interrupted with a collision from Heaven. *For Love's Sake* is not a book about mere adventures into the unknown places of the world. Rather, it is the beginning of a journey. It is the story of lives interrupted by Heaven's touch. This is a literal invitation to be overshadowed by Heaven. This is for *you*.

For Love's Sake is what happens when the reality of Heaven invades normal lives on the earth. It is a heart cry of desperation and hunger for the glory of God to cover the earth as the waters cover the sea. When Heaven touches earth, when love is married to power, nothing can remain the same around it. Everything will change. And one glimpse with the One whose eyes burn with holy love for you will change you forever.

The Moravians—a group that took a life of following Jesus quite literally and began the first modern-day movement of missions and worship—had one cry as they set out running to the ends of the earth: "That the Lamb may receive the reward for His suffering." Their lives were yielded in love for Jesus and a move of the Holy Spirit to flood the earth. Not one lived for himself. After one glance, they were no longer their own but were marked forever as His. There will be more on the Moravians in our conversation. But know that this radical group began the modern movement of mission work in the earth. Their cries of worship rang through the earth unceasingly for one hundred years. Their legacy and heart cries remain in you and me.

This is an invitation into the heart of Jesus. It is the entryway into a lifestyle of outrageous relationship with Jesus where we follow in His footsteps of tangible love and action. It is such a love that is known through encounter. Love that runs with full abandon into the arms of the One it belongs to. It is a call to love, and to love with all that you are.

Enter In

What does it mean to be a carrier of Heaven? We were created to echo Heaven's heartbeat. Can you hear the rhythm? If we listen, we can hear a sound that's familiar to our spirit—the cadence of a dream taking shape. A promise made before time that could only come from outside of ourselves.

Just as Mary partnered with God to bring about a new move of the Spirit in the world—to bring about Jesus, who made a way for us to connect with the Father in a radical way—we now have a new opportunity. Mary's promise made a way for us—*you* and *me*—to partner with Jesus to bring about a greater movement than what the world has ever before witnessed. What am I suggesting? Jesus made it clear that we would do *greater things than these*" (see John 14:12 NIV). That is, we have been given an opportunity to participate in a more massive move of God than even the emergence of Jesus on the world scene!

Biblically speaking, everything in God's Word is ours for the taking. If we can do the same things Jesus did and the same things Mary did, then there are gigantic promises flooding the Bible that are ours to catch, take, and walk out in our own lives. We've been invited to step into the promises of God for our lives, but also to jump into already-paved paths that have been marked by those who have gone before us.

Mary was called to bridge Heaven and earth by bringing life to a new movement of God in the world around her. God saw a humble girl in the dirt—in her ordinary, everyday life setting—and He put His finger on her. Can you envision yourself within her story? One connection with Heaven changed the entire world. Welcome to a journey of being captivated by Heaven's gaze. One that will cost you everything that you possess, but through it, you will gain an inheritance that is too large to carry alone.

Each of us has been given a promise. Like Mary, you have been destined to be overshadowed by the Holy Spirit. What does that look like? Will an angel break into your room at 3 A.M.? Maybe. For all of us, it will be different. God chooses the small, the overlooked, and the nobodies to carry His presence to a dying world. It's not just a great idea. It's who we are.

> *This resurrection life you received from God is not a timid, grave-tending life. It's adventurously expectant, greeting God with a childlike, "What's next, Papa?" God's Spirit touches our spirits and confirms who we really are. We know who He is, and we know who we are: Father and children. And we know we are going to get what's coming to us—an unbelievable inheritance! We go through exactly what Christ goes through. If we go through the hard times with Him, then we're certainly going to go through the good times with Him!* (Romans 8:15-17)

So here's your open door—will you jump in with me?

God places His finger on those of us who are nameless and writes His name on our hearts. He chooses you and me! Mary had no earthly idea what her promise would look like. What would it mean? Yet, she was favored, and her job was simple—she was to say "yes." Your responsibility is not to create your promise or to make it happen. All He is asking for is a willing and empty life, opened up to all that He is. What if you are not empty? Ask God to fill you with all that He is. If we lay all that we are at His feet, He trades us for something much better—God *in* us.

In the end, our cry is to be hidden within His heart, so much so that His reflection forever masks our stares and others in the world around us can see Him in our eyes. To get there, though, is a long journey. It is not necessarily filled with glamour or glitz, but is laid in simplicity and often in the most obscure places that I can describe. This is a journey of capturing a glimpse of what could happen on the earth if little lives would yield to Heaven's hunger.

What am I suggesting? I am convinced that Heaven runs to the hungry because of the hunger that Heaven itself carries.

For Heaven's hunger has a name—it is yours.

Endnotes

1. Ian Morgan Cron, *Chasing Francis: A Pilgrim's Tale* (Colorado Springs, CO: NavPress, 2006), 42.

2. Dr. Rene Padilla, International President, Tearfund International, www.tearfund.org.

Chapter 2

Miracles in the Mud

Now He shall be great to the ends of the earth (Micah 5:4 NKJV).

With nothing but pocket-sized faith, we are setting out. Even our theological boxes will not fit into our backpacks. They are tossed out the window with every other nonessential. Mustard-seed faith—that small, simple belief and expectancy—is ageless. Before we trek on, check inside your own bag. Is it weighed down? Heavy? Are there belongings or "norms" that need to be thrown out, too? All you really need is yourself, a hunger to meet with God, and a willingness to leave the place where you are to get there. (Well, maybe some trail mix and a change of underwear would be helpful, too!)

You might be thinking, "How in the world does a Western girl end up seeing miracles and mayhem and having a run-in with God?" I grew up a small-town girl. I am talking the "one-stoplight-town" kind of girl. There was nothing special about my origin. The first time I heard about miracles was when I inquired about what had happened within my own life. I had no grid for encounters with Jesus—no understanding of what Heaven on earth and "all that jazz" could be about. I was clueless. Miracles were mystical and fantasy. Amidst my everyday life, there was this knowing inside of me that said there had to be something more than what I knew around me. I did not know how to communicate it. It frustrated me! And that frustration started me on a journey of asking questions until I encountered the real-life answers face to face. I simply have not stopped asking.

My hope is that these scribbles of mine will serve as a window or door for you to enter in as well. This odyssey took me through some 22 countries. In it, my companions and I were able to capture a tangible picture of what happens when we choose to step into the reality of Jesus *with* and *in* us— and what can happen if we ask for eyes to see beyond our own pain and the suffering of the world. To see beyond what *is* to what *will be*. The oddity of it all was that most of these sightings of Heaven's touch would not be in the places I had presumed, but on the margins, outside the church walls, and in the outskirts of the earth.

New Eyes

As the airplane skidded during touchdown on the narrow landing strip in Africa, I inhaled a large breath of air as adrenaline blanketed my senses. I had been in Africa a year before—trekking through East Africa through a contact I had found. This time, something was different. Mozambique's northern airport was simple, small, and hidden. As I walked off the small plane, I could hear the sounds of the heart of Africa—the cadence of drums and dancing. It was like a magnet drawing me back to the part of my heart it had captured a year before.

Jumping on the back of a flat-bed truck, I was taken to the place that was to be my home. How long would I be there? I had no idea. The ocean breeze engulfed the air and swept back my hair with a swift flowing current of wind as the truck blasted through the rough roads ahead. We were almost "home"—the place where I would relearn the idea of family.

What were my expectations? I wanted to meet with Jesus—none of the fluff, smoke machines, or ambiance. Resources in technology are great, but I wanted to find something real—a place beyond the touch of human hands. I did not realize that my answer would be more tangible than I had pictured.

The following night, Rolland and Heidi Baker—a pair of renegade missionaries who had entered Mozambique in a time of war and set up homes for children throughout the country and now more than 20 countries around the world—invited me to join them in the bush lands of Mozambique. The Bakers[1] experienced revival like I had never before heard of. Miracles were normal. In places of disaster, they found the supernatural. They have been a living example for me of what can happen when we jump empty-handed into the promises of God in our lives. Today, Mozambique embodies a picture of sustainable revival, the likes of which I have not witnessed elsewhere.

Heidi and Rolland loaded myself, a few other students, and a group of Mozambican fireballs all under the age of ten into a large convoy truck. The ride brought back memories of the dirt-filled air, hills, and wonderful rainbow-colored sunsets that set Africa ablaze with beauty. As we ventured out deeper into the heart of Mozambique's bush, I wondered, "Am I really here?"

As darkness fell on the horizon, the convoy truck came to a bumpy halt. We hopped out of the truck and instantly were greeted by a village of men, women, and children. The rest of the night was a tale in itself, although it was the end when things shifted completely for me.

Heidi was preaching on Jesus' power and invited those who were deaf and blind to come up and be healed. She prayed in Portuguese, *"Vem Espirito*

Santo," inviting the Holy Spirit. I was taken aback by the number of those who came near to be healed. There was no pomp and circumstance—nothing to make what we were doing spectacular. Just us and a desperate need for Jesus to sweep in and do what He does best—to heal us, touch us, and love us back to life.

Heidi saw that there were many who needed to be healed and quickly looked to me and another girl and said, "Pray over this man. He's blind and needs to see." Without as much as a single tangible direction, she scurried back into the African night to pray over some children across the dirt path.

"OK," I thought. Trying to rationalize the erratic situation, I wondered if there was some sort of *How to See the Blind Healed for Dummies* out there somewhere. Maybe I should have stopped at Barnes and Noble before getting on the plane?

The man was led up to us, and there we were—two young women with absolutely no grid for what we were about to encounter. Now, before we move on, the last thing that I would want is for this story to become just another extravagant tale of untainted miracles. I was certainly no super saint. In fact, if I can be completely transparent, I was there without a whole lot of confidence and faith that it would, in fact, manifest before our very eyes.

As I whispered *"Boa noite"* (Good evening) to the man in Portuguese, he smiled. I looked into his large, light blue eyes. Cataracts had taken them over. The white in his eyes was stained with yellow, and extra clear and white tissue covered the rest in large, clumpy layers.

I looked at the girl next to me, and without words, we jumped into the adventure together. I put my hand on the man's shoulder at first. I felt like such a child, so I waited to hear any ounce, any whisper with which Jesus might rescue us. I couldn't seem to hear anything but the sound of my own rapid heart rate that felt like it was about to explode from my chest. With nothing, we prayed, *"Jesus, cura elle. Vem Espirito Santo. Cura."* Jesus, heal this man. Come, Holy Spirit, and heal him.

I peeked out of the corner of my eyes to see if anything was happening. I didn't know if, one, I was feeling God's presence, or two, I was shaking from fear of the unknown that I was immersed within. Either way, we kept praying. And each time, our faith would expand and multiply. Why was that? It was because we were seeing and encountering faith in action right before our very eyes.

As we continued to ask the Holy Spirit to come near us, I remember looking back into the man's eyes. I was shocked at what I saw in front of me. The cataracts and extra tissue covering his large eyes were beginning to fall off—almost seeming to melt away and fall like large, heavy tears down to the African dust in front of him.

"Time out!"

I had never in my life witnessed a blind man seeing! I didn't know if he was getting better or worse. All I knew was that I could feel my pulse about to jump through my veins!

As we watched and waited, the man said he could see some blurry figures. He had not been able to see anything before. I wanted to leap out of my skin! We knew then that something was happening beyond our control or doing. This night was getting interesting!

We prayed again. And each time, more "gunk" would fall from the man's eyes, and those "blurs" would get more defined.

Heidi came over to check on what was happening. She asked the man how he was doing. He said he could actually see some things, but not clearly. That was enough for her. She laughed with joy and said, "Keep praying, he can see better and better!"

A few minutes later, I looked again into the man's eyes, and the bluest of blue became grayish brown. It looked like he had put contacts in. We watched as his eyes went from blue, to gray, to brown. Each time they would change, he could see more and more.

By this time, we did not have to ask how he was doing. He made sure to give an instant update each time. "I can see!" And now, mirrored in his eyes, I could see amazement and wonder shared within our joint stares. What in the world had just happened to us?

I wanted to fall on the ground and collapse in the deep red dirt. Part of me wanted to run in circles. Other parts of me wanted to just cry and thank Jesus. I was in awe and utterly speechless. How on earth was I supposed to react?

As I glanced through the dim lamplight—which was really a tiny light bulb hanging from the truck with a tattered rope we had with us—I could see Heidi praying over a few children about ten feet away. Suddenly I heard, *"Yesu."*[2] A little girl was mute from birth, and I was there to witness her first word as she was completely healed—"Jesus."

The village was in complete amazement. Many people came running just to know this Jesus who could heal the ones they loved.

I sat there on the back of the truck riding home and shook under the wonder that I had encountered. While I assumed great complexity in the evening, Jesus saw simplicity. He came running to the dirt. All we had to do was call His name. It was that simple.

Traveling back home, as the wind flooded my senses with a force that seemed to reform the skin on my face, I looked up through a hole in the truck covering and saw the countless stars of Africa. It was a window, a door of invitation to me.

I heard only a whisper that night, "Come run with Me. There's so much more that you haven't seen. Just come with Me; take My hand."

My answer was simple: "Okey dokey, Jesus. Let's go."

In a matter of mere minutes, my world would be turned upside down. Perhaps it was to shake the things out of me that would not fit into a child-like existence. As I close my eyes, I can still see that man, those eyes, and that dim lamp light above us. A blind man could now see. And gazing back,

I am still not sure what the greatest miracle was. Was it the blind man's miracle, or my own? I didn't know it then, but I was learning to see as well and finding out just how blind I had once been.

An Open Door

The heat of the night in Africa's summer takes your breath away. I lay on my bed, and through my mosquito net I could see the moonlight on the ocean nearby on the horizon. Randi was lying in her bed directly across from mine. Randi was an outgoing girl from Pennsylvania with the accent to prove it. We met as students in a mission school there in Mozambique. Having both traveled to Africa for the same reason—to meet with Jesus— we soon realized that we shared similarities in our heart's pursuit. Somehow, we would end up a team, and later best friends. Our shared odyssey began with a night to remember.

We had been in Mozambique for three months, and both Randi and I were scheduled to depart and return to the United States in two short weeks. The past three months had been filled with encounters with Jesus that marked me forever, some that are beyond words or description. Yet, something inside of me was frustrated.

Under the massive orange and yellow moon, I made my way to the ocean in the distance. The feeling of sand between my toes and the smell of the ocean tide made my senses come alive. The moonlight was on the water as I watched in stillness for some kind of answer. I wasn't quite sure what I was looking for. But I was soon caught up into a different world entirely while sitting there on the water's edge.

Have you ever been given an amazing gift from someone and all you wanted to do was rip the wrapping off and use it? Remember when you were a little kid? Christmas morning would come and you couldn't wait to tear through the paper to get to the prize you had been dreaming of for months on end. Remember the feeling you got when you played with that new toy for the very first time?

Those were the very feelings that were conjured up in me that night. I had been given this amazing gift—an invitation into the heart of God for the earth. A door to a Kingdom that was so very foreign to me inside and out, and in reality had been swung wide open the entire time. It was an offer to take Jesus' hand and see what He sees, feel what He feels, go where He goes. Yet, as the tide inched its way toward me that night, impatience seemed to sit next to me as my closest friend.

I stayed in the wet sand waiting for something—anything. I felt like I had that "something" in front of me, but didn't know how to use it. I didn't know the how or where or what or why. I just knew in my heart that there was something more than what I could see with my eyes. It was something that would be found in a place farther away than I had ever been before. The questions that lingered in my mind were, "How do I get there?" "Where exactly is 'there' anyway?" and "Where can I get the key?"

Living with unanswered questions is a sticky process. At least it is for me. Think of Mary's situation! How awkward would her story have been? When the angel left, she would be alone, mulling over what had just crashed into her life from nowhere. Where was she supposed to go from there? What next? And how would she explain something so upside down?

Is There Room?

The angel had just left. She had said, "Yes." Yet in her willingness came questions from all four winds.

"OK," she thought, "God is going to live *in* me? What on earth does that look like?"

She had no idea how to communicate what had happened and what would happen in the near future. Why was she chosen? How would she accomplish this? Was it all a mistake? Maybe she just had eaten too much for dinner? But even late-night snacking could not make this unbelievably real dream come to life. In her attempt to rationalize the holy chaos invading her life, she must have wondered again—was she simply dreaming?

In the fog of her encounter, Mary began to ponder. And that pondering would echo throughout the rest of her life.

How do you become a carrier of God in the world around you? Mary's "yes" would become the fulcrum of the greatest expression of Heaven on earth that the world had ever known. In the first-ever "Christmas" present, Mary would unwrap the existence of Glory Himself in the dirt around her—the literal embodiment of her God-breathed dream come to life right in front of her very eyes.

The question was, "Would there be room for Him?"

Well, you guessed it. The world did not make room—it just wasn't prepared for His emergence. Imagine her frustration. The angel promised that everything was possible with God. He spoke favor over Mary, and yet she found herself giving birth for the first time in a cave surrounded by animals, in a most obscure place in the heart of Israel. Picture in your mind's eye her thinking process.

In the midst of chaos and a crazy road trip with her husband, would come her answer.

A Naked King

The smells of the livestock cave were breathtaking—literally. She was exhausted. This was her first shot at motherhood, but she'd have to wing it. As her breathing intensified, Joseph knocked on every hotel for a room, but all the vacancy signs were dimmed.

Wonderful, right? Was this how Heaven was supposed to rip through the realm of humanity? What about the angel and the encounter that seemed so thick and theatrical? Was God really going to burst forth in the dirt? Was

His "grand" entrance going to be meager and lowly? Was it going to come naked and raw? That doesn't seem very regal, does it?

What do you think was going on in this young woman's mind?

"You've got to be *kidding* me. I've carried God inside of me for nine grueling months, been on a road trip of disastrous proportions, and to top it all off, I smell like a donkey from head to toe. And this is the way I am going to experience the reality of the angel's promise to me—in a cave, on the ground, with nothing to usher Him in?"

Was this how Jesus—who the angel told her would have a throne and a Kingdom that would never end—was to arrive on the world scene? And how would He come? Through pain like she had never before known. That's right, ladies, there was no epidural. Mary would kick this *old school*.

Through Mary's suffering would come immense joy. That was the divine promise. The road there, though, would prove longer than she had expected. I wonder if that is the same with each of us. Can you see yourself in this reflection?

Mary's story began as an unexpected break-in from Heaven. Think about it. The angel didn't even knock! Within her story and in our own lives, there are striking parallels and patterns.

Usually it begins with our open door and invitation. Jesus does this in a multitude of ways. For me, it meant showing up in my bedroom—albeit uninvited—so many years ago. What does your life look like? How do you meet with God? How has He crashed into your life? Is He trying now?

From there—after He speaks these incredible promises of what He is going to do in the earth and shares with you that *you* actually get to go with Him—things do not always turn out the way we originally plan. When an encounter happens and you see in His eyes a reflection of yourself, everything changes. For me, I think I expected a fairy tale of sorts. Growing up watching Disney princesses such as Snow White and Cinderella, I pictured Jesus as this grand guy who would sweep in on a white horse and take me to "Never Never Land" or whatever magical kingdom He belonged to. My framework was not connected with the reality of His Kingdom, which was so very foreign to me.

My transportation would not be a white stallion, but rickety buses, camels, and, most often, my dirt-covered feet! The kingdom I would find would not be filled with diamonds, pizza, and fondue fountain, but rather rice, beans, and mud huts. The dwellings that He would actually take me to would not be paved with "golden brick roads" but dirt-covered paths. And sometimes there were no paths at all!

As with Mary, God wants to do insane exploits in the earth. Sadly, many times there is no room for Him in our lives. It is so very upside down that most of us aren't willing to stand on our heads to see it. Thankfully, Jesus always has a way of getting you there anyway.

When God visits you, things begin to transform. He gives us eyes to see an entirely different view and impregnates us—just as He did Mary—with the very heartbeat of Heaven.

The Ultimate Break-In

Let's look at Mary as the limited young woman that she was. A simple girl in the dirt, minding her own business—a preoccupied gal preparing for a wedding to the one she loved. So we know the girl was busy, right? She most definitely had a plan for her life. At least we know that her family would have had expectations for her future that complemented the culture around her.

Eagerly, God looked on and saw one who ravished His heart. And, in His usual way, He couldn't contain His excitement and broke in unannounced. This birthing in Mary of a new move of God in the earth would change her entire life even before the moment of its conception. The moment of choice was when her life would shift entirely.

There would be an immense cost. She could be stoned as an unmarried, pregnant teenager. Think of the reproach of such a thing in our day. How much more would she have to answer to in her own time? She knew these facts well enough in her culture. The ramifications of choosing to say "yes" were numerous.

Her family probably wouldn't understand. Frankly, how could they? How would you feel if your already-lovestruck teenage daughter came up to you one morning and said, "Mom, Dad, umm. Well, last night an angel came to my room. Yeah, I know, that's weird. I know it sounds crazy, but it happened. His light was so bright. He said I would become pregnant before I am married. I asked him how and he said God would overshadow me. He also said that the baby would be God Himself. The baby is going to be King and will have a throne that will last forever! Pretty cool, huh? So, what do you think? Is that OK with you?"

Looking at it that way brings a whole new perspective, doesn't it? Can you see your reflection in Mary's life? What is your promise? What is it that you see as you stare into His eyes? Can you feel Heaven's heartbeat inside of you? Forget the unknowns. What is it that you know within you to be unshakably true?

Mary faced demeaning glares, persecution, immense physical pain and heartache, and a nationwide attempt to extinguish her life and that of her family. She became a refugee and crossed national borders with a newborn. She had absolutely no grid for what was to come or how to walk out her promise. There were no *What to Expect When You're Expecting the Son of God* guides on the city bookshelves. She would have to learn how to protect her promise one day at a time. And one day give it up, only to find it again.

Whispers on the Water

Randi and I lay awake toward the end of school and talked about life. We'd had these encounters with Jesus that had rocked our world. But we didn't have an inkling of how to walk them out in our everyday lives. We didn't fit the molds we had been shown before. Soon we would find out why.

Standing in the wet sand, still waiting for some twinkle of a star, tidal wave, or something tangible to speak to me, I stared out on the water. My eyes fell on the moonlit path that stretched the span of its length—flowing over as if running off the side of the earth—in front of me. There was such peace in the movement on the waters that night, such meditation, and it instantly spurred my curiosity. Sitting there in stillness, I heard, "Your time is not up yet. Stay close to Me. Just listen one day at a time. You don't have to know what it looks like and you don't have to have a grand plan. I have something to show you and give you here in Africa. I'll go with you. Will you go with Me?"

My rationalization skills quickly set in. What in the world was happening? Maybe I was dehydrated? I had no idea. Did I need special permission to live this kind of lifestyle? But then again, what did I have to lose? I decided at that moment to run with God's voice. Or, in this case, run with Him wherever He would take me.

I ran back to our room and burst in unannounced, shouting, "I'm staying in Africa. I'm not leaving—I found my answer!" Randi was in our clustered, confined room getting ready to go to sleep, and without so much as a breath, replied, "I'm staying too. Let's do it. Can we really go after what we've heard from God? Do you think it will work?" As if searching for some invisible form of "permission," we took turns sharing our heart and the dreams that we had received while listening to Jesus in our times alone.

Where would we go? How would we get there? Where would we stay? How would we pay for it? We hadn't the faintest notion. But we were so incredibly buzzed at the thought of truly living out what we had dreamed—a radical relationship with Jesus—that we didn't have time to care. We had our eyes on a promise that we couldn't possibly create ourselves—an undertaking that found its genesis beyond our capabilities and who we were. Our heart's cry would be sealed in another encounter with none other than the One who seems to love the dirt more than we do.

Give Your Life Away

It all began in the place where we spent most of our time—on the floor, or in this context, the dirt. The thick African air was heavy that day, and we were not alone.

The thin green and yellow banana leaf mat beneath me served as my only refuge from the strange and complex mixture of garbage, sand, and insects that engulfed the world at life in the sand below. There was nothing glamorous about this encounter. No glitter, no glitz; just the mud and a few (and by few, I mean massive quantities of) African flies swarming in the air around us. Yet there remains beauty in the moments when Jesus walks in unexpected and forever shatters my tiny box of theological assumptions.

In my meager attempt at giving my life away, at becoming a sacrifice, at laying my life on an altar, I realized something. "We are all called to this same altar."[3] It is the one that dates back to the days in the dust where God told Abraham to do the unthinkable and give up everything he had—his promised son. It is the same table that countless heroes of faith throughout time all had to climb upon willingly. On that altar are the remains of lives given away for love. It is not a fancy, gold-plated façade of Heaven. It is a sturdy, raw reality of laid-down love, a place where our sacrifice makes way for others to come.

Back in that moment, I was face down in the dirt. Jesus just cannot help but run and dive face-first with us in those times of surrender. He was there! In majesty and simplicity He was there. In suffering and joy, the fullness of both, I am telling you—He was there!

Caught somewhere between being set before His face and being pressed against the ground, I could hear the worship rising around us. My heart leaped as hundreds worshiped under a dilapidated tent with more holes than actual canvas. As I closed my eyes, I could feel a thickness in the air around me. It was as if Jesus was walking all around us—in the midst of dirt, bugs, sweat, garbage, and all.

The atmosphere under the large tent soon carried an awareness of Jesus next to us. When I opened my eyes, I watched as children began to fall to the ground under that thick presence. Tears streamed down their faces as they wept and shook uncontrollably. As worship continued, a large gust of wind blew into the tent, and I found myself beside these little ones in the same condition.

These moments defined what I came to expect in the coming days. The environment was not what I was used to. There were no lighting effects, no fancy equipment, and certainly no cushy chairs or even carpet! Face first in the dirt, I began to see the reality that I had been searching for—I was meeting with God in the most unusual and unexpected of places.

I came to Africa nearly a year before for one purpose—to find Jesus. I needed to know that He was who He said He was. Where I had come from, I was served a picture of a "Jesus" that mirrored society around me. A "Jesus" who was too impeccably clean and polished to make His way to the dirt—the messiness of our lives—let alone stay there. It was an image whose slogan could echo Burger King's famous line: "Have it your way." Or in this case, "Have *Him* your way."

Our Jesus was coming just to be with us, in the mud and all. No hype or incantation was needed to entice Him.

Hours later, music filled the tent as worship continued. That day, Cindy Ruakere, an amazing worship warrior woman from New Zealand, was playing a song called "Receive." In it she sings,

> "That the Lamb may receive the reward for His suffering
> That the Lamb may receive His reward through me
> Only by grace will this ever be done
> To lay my life down as a gift from the Son
> And to the lamb who stands among us as King
> I give up my life as an offering."[4]

As the song filled the air, I found myself on the dirt-covered banana leaf mats that (sort of) covered the dirt. I wanted to give everything that I possessed—all that I was—to God in that moment. I was mystified at the "how" of doing it.

As my eyes were closed, I heard, "Will you give your life away?" What did that mean? I wasn't sure, but in the midst of a tremendous move of the Holy Spirit, it was pretty hard to say "no." I did know one thing—I couldn't just stay where I was. I wanted all of Him and everything He had for my life. But first, He was asking for all of me with no questions asked.

"Receive" became the song that filled the melody of our lives and launched us into parts of the earth we had only imagined.

My heart's cry was "yes." This "yes" cry is where our journey begins.

The Vault of Heaven

I bet you're thinking, "Does this really happen?" Take some time and position your heart to encounter the answer for yourself. Come with me, for this is what we have all been created for. Above and beyond career, personal goals, and family expectations lies a deep longing to live life in a most profound way. The way that is unpaved, bumpy, and, quite frankly, can be offensive to those on Main Street or Wall Street. It is the way of complete and utter abandonment into the arms of the One who will do the rest.

The thrilling part is that we can get there as easily as calling His name. Why do we feel the need to complicate it, create an atmosphere for it, or strive to enter it? This place is where Jesus gains access into our lives in a massive way. In His eyes will be all you need. They will speak to you beyond words and show you a reflection of yourself that you might not have seen before. In those moments, the barriers we see in front of our lives and our destinies will quickly fade away. Sounds awfully simple, don't you think? Welcome to a life of relearning the ways of childlike faith.

Regardless of whether you are in a country that abounds in wealth, megachurches, and Christian bookstores, or if you reside in one with huts, open-air markets, and mosques, without God's presence, nothing matters. Without His hand, you can do nothing. And why would you want to, anyway?

Some people will search for the face of Jesus in training centers, schools, seminaries, goals, ambitions, or even people whom they've elevated into "superstar" status. We were made to love and to never stop. Of course, we know we have much to learn from those who have gone before us. And resources such as books and conferences are a great key to furthering our pursuit of living life in His heart.

Where do you and I search Him out? Do we seek Jesus in familiar places—in church only on Sundays—or is our God big enough to invade our Mondays as well? What if it were as simple as making room for Him in our hearts? What if God could come be with us, no matter what our environment and surroundings looked like? What if it were so simple that a child could hear it and run with it?

Heidi always says she has known children under the age of ten who can preach better than the most famous of ministers in the Western world. Why is that? It was because they were hungry. They asked Jesus to come. And— wait for it…wait for it—He did!

So the children began to teach me. "Jesus, come…Jesus, come…." The more I cried out, the hungrier I would become. It wasn't brain surgery, but the results of an eternal promise that had pulsated through all realms and all ages. He came near to be with us. He always comes.

Let me lay it all on the table for you now. Learning to love is messy and hard. It hurts. Living in the shadow of Jesus is much more than throwing a dollar bill at a beggar or starting a project to feed the hungry. Sure, that stuff counts, but that is just the beginning. Learning to love means giving our lives. It will cost us something. If it doesn't, what are we doing, anyway? We are all going to spend our lives, pay our lives out for something. Why not let it become for the embodiment of love itself?

This lifestyle of love is more than philanthropy. It is more than who we are and our own strength. We cannot do it without His help. There are too many needs. There are too many diseases. Too much hurt and pain and hunger and death around us. Money is not the answer, and we are not the answer to the world around us. We are a part of creation that desperately needs help, too! Knowing we are a mess ourselves coupled with the power of a life broken will change things around us. We need Jesus in order to love like He loves. We need His hands to see the sick healed. We need His heart to love in a dying world. He is the answer that we are so desperately in need of. Reaching out our hands can change today. Living in His presence will transform tomorrow.

There is much more to see in the depths of God's heart. God longs to show it to us. He hungers to reveal to us all of His deep plans. He desires to share with us all the rooms in His house. His joy is in you and me just being His kids. He is not just the Western Jesus. He embraces the entire world, desperately seeking His borderless Bride.

Jesus is pursuing us with a radical love. His love can cause your world and the world around you to be turned upside down. Mary's promise was coming in a way she did not expect, in simplicity and obscurity. Oftentimes, the very thing God places inside of us will be rejected by the natural order in the environment around us. God embraces the impossible—the unnatural. He breaks through what is naturally possible and shows us what can happen when we have His grace and power in our everyday existence. There is a reproach to carrying God in a way that has never before been done in recorded history—a cost that will touch our lives in many ways. There will be no grid or pattern to rely on. But in those places, He comes close and reminds us that we are not alone.

His question echoes through time to all of us—what is our cry? Our heart's cry will answer His. Will you say "yes" to the promises of God that are within your life?

Endnotes

1. Rolland and Dr. Heidi Baker are founders and directors of Iris Ministries, Inc., www.iris-min.org.

2. The word *Yesu* means "Jesus" in the tribal language of Makua.

3. Lesley-Anne Leighton, director, Holy Given International School of Missions, www.holygiven.org.

4. "Receive," written and sung by Cindy Ruakere, www.cindyruakere.com.

Chapter 3

Heaven's Heartbeat

For in Him we live and move and have our being (Acts 17:28 NIV).

The enemy of true life has a way of tricking us into hinging our existence on half-truths—ideas that seem noble, but in the end rob us of the fullness that we were created to live within. The "shoulda coulda wouldas" of days gone by trap us in yesterday—the past—or our cultural collective past. The constant pressures for undefined and abstract "success" hurl us into the future through the constant demand for more and the consistent push for "higher" living. All the while, today is forgotten, overlooked, and becomes a mere gateway toward something better—or so we think. Caught somewhere between the past and the future are our todays, ticking quickly by us. Have we been tricked into giving our lives away for falsehood? What do you give yourself to? Why do you do what you do?

Living in the "now" of our lives is a sometimes-overlooked reality. Being present in the moment of God's interaction in our daily lives helps us to see the distinguishing that God makes known between the light and the darkness in the environments around us.

Western consumerist culture strives to be a seeker of truth. We look for it everywhere. We invest our lives into this search. In Buddhism today, a strong emphasis is made on living in the moment, the now, and being present in our lives. Multitudes of people are drawn to this concept, but many of us do not realize that it is a mere counterfeit exercise of a divine truth handed down by God, the Father of Jesus.

There are many seekers in the world who have encountered the Christian faith and have left with scars and a hefty and terrible taste in their mouths. They have essentially "thrown the baby out with the bath water" and gone after fakes and half-truths. It is true that the Western Church has been tainted with outside agendas of allegiance. History then and now has documented our mistakes quite legibly. But even in our mistakes there is hope.

Within each culture, including the American one, God leaves His fingerprint. Culture in and of itself is beautiful and God-ordained. Our job is to extract the precious from the vile. We cannot throw away the intentions of God for a land. Instead, we bless it and latch onto what is good and from His heart.

Baby Steps

Have you ever awoken and realized that you are in an enchanting place where spirit, soul, and body are attuned to the reality of Heaven on earth that you thought could only *possibly* exist in a sugarplum dreamland? That's the very feeling that emanated around me this particular morning in my story. Just a few years ago, I had been living a "normal," run-of-the-mill life. I was doing what I was supposed to, according to societal norms. I was setting goals for my own selfish ambitions and striving with all of my might to "be" somebody, to measure up, and to "reach the stars," even if they were the fake plastic glow-in-the-dark ones that someone secretly stuck on my bedroom ceiling! I was spending my life on things that were fading away, and I wondered, "Why?"

That morning, I found myself surrounded in the midst of sweat and the sand that had blown through my window, creating an outline of myself like a crime scene chalk drawing as I arose. I knew that I had found a place where my dreams really could come true. It wasn't a fairy tale, but it was more tangible than what I could touch, see, and feel around me.

That dawning would be the beginning of a wandering that no one on earth could prepare me for. In fact, if you had told me what would happen in the months to come, I wouldn't have believed you.

Let me take you there—to our baby steps into a very upside-down Kingdom.

Learning to Walk

As Randi and I boarded the plane, we were inebriated with expectancy. It was our fuel. I looked down and saw my meager pair of flip-flops and a small backpack of clothes and sundries. We had nothing to make something happen in the places where God was sending us. We possessed no props, no brightly colored lights. Not even a *Jesus* video, hilariously enough! All we knew was to take one step at a time. God would provide whatever He needed for us to reach the people He was sending us to.

Imagine nearly two millennia ago—the day when Jesus took His first steps; those first moments of learning how to speak, how to eat, even potty training. Do we ever see Jesus in this light?

The King of kings brought nothing with Him as He entered the world as fully human—naked and dependent. Think about it. Jesus left glory for the dirt. He would come as a newborn, in weakness and fragility. He would have to learn to walk in the world He was sent to. He came to learn, and most of the time we find Him living, learning, and loving on the margins. Just as His followers today are called to do.

When Jesus invites us to step into His big shoes and dance with Him— to enter into an outrageous relationship with Him on the earth—it can be a little wobbly at first. Or in our case, it can be *very* wobbly. We learned as we entered the country of Tanzania just how much we needed Him.

Arriving in the city of Dar Es Salaam, a flashback of a year earlier played before me. I had been in the city before and recognized the urban features around us. I remembered the dancing, the joy, all in one view. The familiar sights, the smells, the sounds. The rhythm of life was in full swing around us. It was the sheer excitement and anticipation of the unknown.

Filling out our paperwork at the visa checkpoint, we were approached by a government official with the sobering news that we were denied an entry visa into Tanzania. As we asked why, we were told this decision was made because we didn't have a ticket out of the country.

The officer went back to his office and came back a few minutes later. As he got near, I addressed him respectfully in Kiswahili. *"Shikamoo bwana. Habari za asubuhi?"* Greetings sir. How are you this morning?

You would have thought with the look in his eyes that he had seen an alien or some foreign thing (which, I guess, is technically true)! His shock turned into curiosity as he comprehended my greeting. Not only would this same official override the denial of our visas and grant us entry, he would also grant us multiple entries into Tanzania, which is highly irregular. Our conversation that followed turned out to be full of intrigue. He wanted to know why we were here. We were just asking the same question! The only sense we could make of it was that God had called us to this place and put the people of this nation on our hearts.

These moments were our proverbial first steps into a place we knew little about. As wonky as our little feet were, we felt such a joy on Jesus' face. The same face that a Father makes when He sees the best of Himself in the one that He has created. It was a picture that would sustain us through nearly two dozen countries.

A Divine Cadence

A little time had passed since Mary was informed of the impossible taking place in her life. She would be reminded of that purpose in a most tangible way. After the grasping of our promise—the beginning of going after our destiny—the initial energy and excitement can begin to wear down. In its place come questions from every area of our lives.

As she stared outside of the house as the busyness of the day was beginning to wind down, another event would suddenly happen. This morning would bring Mary's first sneak peek into her promise—a new movement of God in the earth. She would literally feel these "movements" as the days flew by.

At first, she thought it could have been jitters, but this feeling within her was different. She had been waiting for the embodiment of what the angel had spoken to her. Then, there it was—the first kick. If John the Baptist would leap with joy inside of Elizabeth's womb, how much more would the Son of God dance inside of Mary?

There it was again—a kick. Imagine when the baby turned, and Mary held her hand on her stomach. Picture in your mind's eye this moment when she did, as a pulsating rhythm began to beat in a way that made melody to her ears, piercing deep in her spirit.

Her promise was growing, and although she must have been afraid and unsure of what would come next, she continued to say yes. Through the moments of physical exhaustion and pain, she would push through. In her times of fear of the unknown and questioning her physical provision and safety, she pressed on. In the times of great reproach—when her family and society around her might not have understood—still the girl moved with the rhythm she now heard and felt within her.

Mary was realizing that her dream was alive and she was living it. The first signs of life in our promises and destinies are where what has been promised to us begins to take shape and manifest within us. In these times we can feel the literal overshadowing from Heaven tangibly within ourselves, in our spirit's quickening us to what we have been destined to walk in.

In the coming days, when her life would prove more overwhelming than ever before, Mary was reminded by a single kick—a single movement—that God's presence was always with her. He was doing a work inside of her that would transform the world around her as never before. It would all be worth it in the end.

That pulsating rhythm Mary felt inside of her was the heartbeat of Heaven. As she nurtured her dream within her, those ripples and beats would grow stronger and more intense as her promise would be birthed in the earth.

Hidden Treasures

What were our first signs of life in the dream God had put in us? I'm glad you asked. Hold on tight now, for this ride is one that goes from the moment you get on and really never stops or ends. It is a lifelong ride. The first signals to us in the birth of our promises were emerging in the eyes of the people He would send us to and the presence that He would send of Himself each time we asked.

We had no idea at the time why we were in Tanzania, but we would gain a treasure that would be more valuable than the richest of gems—the simplicity of the good news. The true good news that is alive in the world around us. Good news looks like something. To the hungry, good news looks like food. To the thirsty, it is embodied in water. To the orphan, good news looks like entering adoption into a family. It is more than words. Good news is the answer to our specific emptiness and need— body, soul, and spirit.

The air around the city was thick. Coughing that night, I swore I had a "hair ball" or "dust ball" in my throat. Dar Es Salaam was a very large city on the coast of Tanzania. Bedbugs were attacking Randi's legs and mine in a fiery ambush. The sounds from the mosques of prayers in the form of song and cries five times a day created a constant ambiance of noise around us.

Arriving in Tanzania, we had witnessed God open doors that were once closed before us. Even with the provision thus far, we needed shelter—a place to stay. A year before, while in East Africa, I had met an amazing Maasai woman named Bella. I had known her in a city far from where we now were, on the other end of the massive country. Somehow, when we arrived, she was living there on Tanzania's east coast.

Bella arranged for Randi and I to stay with Sophia, a beautiful Tanzanian widow, and her three daughters. We would become part of their family. God was opening doors that we couldn't possibly begin to jar, let alone keep open. And what came next shattered all of our expectations.

Getting Low

The look of perplexity on the pastor's face alerted us to the idea that we definitely were not what they had been expecting. Sophia had spoken of us in her church as women who had seen great miracles and power.

Looking down at us, the tall pastor asked, "Are these the ones you had spoken of?" As if he were expecting to see the two witnesses from Revelation in front of him!

When Sophia confirmed that we were in fact the ones, Pastor Swai began to voice his thinking aloud.

"I was expecting old women with years of experience by the sound of your stories—or apostles at the very least. I didn't expect a couple of young girls."

In the silence that followed his reflections, I giggled. Yes, that's right, I laugh when I'm nervous. It can be either a great gift or a terrible weakness, depending on the situation and your perspective. The look in Randi's eyes as she intently glared at me said it all: "Great job *slick*. We're in more trouble now."

After a few moments together, Pastor Swai looked down again at us and over his glasses said, "Well, we want what you have. You will minister at the next service. See you then."

OK, you can say it with me. Whew!

"Called to the Altar"[1]

We awoke early in the morning to make it across town to the church. As we walked in, we were dumbfounded by the number of people that were waiting. Over a thousand people crowded the large open-air structure.

When asking Jesus what I should say, I felt empty. I knew all I could give was what I had received. As worship came to a close and I was asked up to the platform, a small whisper brushed through my ears, "You can do nothing without Me. Get low and worship. Pray until My presence comes. Do not begin to speak until I am there among you."

With that being my only direction, I got down on the stone floor. My knees were shaking from knowing that God was actually going to come and be with us, or maybe it was from the fear that I was completely wrong!

It was as if a wave of God's presence began to capsize the crowd. As we worshiped, I could feel a deep hunger in my spirit to see the reality of Jesus among us. We needed real bread, a real heavenly encounter.

I invited the large crowd to ask Him to come be with us together. The sound was deafening as over a thousand people began to cry aloud for more of His presence. We didn't want or need anything else. We just needed Him, here and now. Like little kids, we had one focus—we needed our Jesus. We wanted Him. And we got what our hearts so desperately desired.

I didn't know what would happen next. As I looked up from the floor, I could see a rushing cloud of God's presence that began in the back. People were falling to the floor, overwhelmed by the answer to our cries.

Steadily, the wave of God's presence made its way to the front. The room was being taken over by Heaven's agenda, not our own. I looked over, beginning to speak while still on the floor, and realized my interpreter was knocked to the ground by the power of God. I had no insight for how to react. There is no "how-to" guide of what to do when God invades our lives and certainly no seminary classes that covered this in my formal training. I was in awe—the kind of feeling that seems to stop time dead in its tracks. Looking over the crowd of people, I saw a hunger that I had only seen a few times before.

"Jesus, help please!" I prayed. What do you say when Jesus is walking right by you? I was desperate. This really was holy chaos!

From the floor I could hear the sounds of weeping and laughing all in one sound. I wanted to stay in this place forever. No words were needed. The look on His face would say it all. How can you describe colliding into the One who is altogether worthy? That heavy presence is what I live for.

If we will get low, He will come. For some mysterious reason, Jesus loves the low place—the place that is full of hunger and humility, a place of emptiness and total dependence. It is a place where ambition flees and fullness abounds and where we, together, realize our need.

The uncreated One dives face-first into the realm of humanity and stays, lingers until we are full. What happened that day? Without a word, children began to give their lives away to Jesus. Around the altar were little ones laid out as gifts to Someone who would come be with them in the sufferings of life and bring them joy.

Soon, adults followed in the footsteps of the young. We watched as Jesus showed us what He could do if we, without decoration, offered our little lives to Him. In a flash, I saw Heaven storm our lives, capturing the hearts of those who were willing to take a chance and enter in.

It's not complicated. The door is open not just to the "bigwigs" and the "rock stars" whom we've elevated in our own minds and circles. This is for us, too—for me and for you. It's a pledge for the nobodies, the weak, and the overlooked in society today. It is based on the sidelines where God chooses those of us who have once been left out. In fact, it's a guarantee and vow.

Can life really look like this, you ask? I found out pretty quickly that it could and would. What would change if we got low and invited Heaven to seize our lives completely? What would transpire if we just said yes to God's plans for our lives?

Kwaherini (Good-bye)

That night I awoke in a fog of what had happened the morning before. "Did that really occur before our eyes? Maybe I was dreaming?" At the home of Pastor Swai, we were introduced as *dadas*—sisters in their family.[2] Mama Swai is one of the warmest women I have ever met. As we sat down for dinner that night, she heaped mounds of rice and goat meat on our plates. We were positive that our stomachs would not have the capacity for all of this goodness.

As I muse on those fleeting days, I miss her gentle smile. Pictures flash through my heart of times of laughter together. Washing the laundry with nothing but a lone rock and our hands and strong embraces that smashed our rosy cheeks against hers. Memories of times when, like a little child, I would read in Swahili aloud, looking up and seeing her nod of approval and glee. Glancing back, those memories seem so distant. Yet, when I close my eyes, I am there once more.

Pastor and Mama Swai said good-bye to us with hands in ours. In their eyes, I could see affirmation. I was blindsided by their deep love and welcoming spirits. We were no longer strangers, but invited to step into the family. In leaving, Pastor Swai had one final word of assessment. Looking down at us as a grandfather could only do, he said, "You've been called to Africa. You carry with you fire. Better keep going. Little girls? I didn't expect it, and I don't get it." This time, he was the one giggling.

Jesus never comes in the packages we expect. He really does use the weak to make the wise wonder in amazement. I still visit the Swais often, each time learning the extent of the treasure we had been given.

Living, Learning, and Loving

The next morning Sophia dropped us off at the noisy and crowded bus station. We were in store for an eight-hour bus ride to the north central part of Tanzania. Our destination: the foot of Mount Kilimanjaro.

As the bus came to a stop, we realized that the eight-hour estimated time of arrival was really a complete myth. It would become much longer than we had been sold. Jolted by the uneven roads, we looked at each other and laughed at the realization that what we now were a part of was real life and more than the theoretical dream it had been before.

The scenery around us was lush and green. I scanned the scenery in contemplation as we brushed past the heart of the country. Huts lined the sides of the road, and barefoot children were giggling and running alongside with eyes so wide and full of wonder that they seemed to contain eternity. And the thought jumped in my mind, "Why in the world would God give me this extravagant gift? This life? Why me? Why us?"

I looked over at Randi bumping up and down as the bus rode faster and faster. She had this look in her eyes of astonishment. We were really here. This was our life. And it had just begun.

We had absolutely no understanding of how and where to go from there. We were made aware that this manifestation around us—the miracles, the people, the way of life in general in Africa—was a kingdom where only the childlike could see and navigate clearly. And we were in need of help every step of the way. The next leg on the road before us would be in a village that would forever sear itself as a defining moment in my life.

Likamba Village

The colors in the sky, ground, and air around the village were so very vibrant and deep that they seemed to pass beyond natural capability. The hues were so striking that they looked like they were bursting at the seams with color, reminding me of the run-in with Heaven that I had had with Jesus when I encountered beauty beyond description. It startled me seeing the same dynamic color in real ordinary life. This was a place of such life and carried within it swirls of hope and laughter. From the sounds of children ringing throughout the hills to the sweeping gusts of wind, there was a shift inside of my spirit as I stepped back into the dirt of Likamba village.

Stepping back onto the rich red dirt in Likamba, I was taken back to memories of my literal first steps in Africa. Those first movements had brought me back full-circle to the beginning.

As we came to the small home in the heart of the village, I recognized Pastor Elirehema. I had met Elirehema and his family a couple years beforehand. If I could give you a simple picture in one condensed package, one of my favorite memories with Elirehema is when he would take me back and forth from the village on his motorbike.

Before the new mode of transportation, we had walked for about two hours to get to where they lived. Allow me to let you in on yet another secret. I am dreadfully awful at directions! I thought I knew the way each time, and convinced everyone else that I did as well. Don't you know it, every time we got lost!

One day after hiking this trek yet again, Elirehema looked at me and, in his usual nature, laughed. Not a little laugh, but a loud, belly laugh. I asked him why he was laughing, and he pointed to his motorbike near the hut!

He was brimming with hilarity at the irony of my elongated journey to his home. He was right, this land—Africa that is—was still very foreign to me. I had so much more to learn.

I am still not sure what was more exhausting—walking four hours round trip to Likamba and back, or hanging on for dear life on the back of that motorbike as it ramped off of dirt hills and cliffs eroded from rain and other natural events! In any case, there we all were together again—Randi, myself, Elirehema, Mama Juliet (his wife), and his family—and instantly able to continue where we had left off.

Likamba village had grown to be an Eden of sorts for us—a place of beginning and immense growth and fruitfulness in our lives. There was such simplicity and joy there. Randi and I walked up to the nursery school that afternoon. Children were being let out and running en masse toward us.

The sun was shining, leaving nothing untouched. The sky was more blue than I thought was possible. With the contrast of the tall, green, lush grass, rich red dirt, and rolling mountainsides, it made me whisper a little prayer under my breath. "God, please let Heaven be like this!"

A Motive of Reversal

I am keenly aware that in writing about mission work or supernatural living in deep places within the earth, there is this expectancy to read extravagant exploits in the most dangerous of places, some of which are a part of our story. There is also this urge in us that needs to perform, or justify what God is doing in and around us. We want to hear these, don't we? They do happen—those times when the presence of Jesus is so thick around us that it spins our heads or leaves us frozen in awe.

What about the little moments though? Are we quick to overlook them or judge them as meaningless and void of power? Truth be told, the times that have changed my life the most have not been while in a church or ministering, even when people were being healed and God's presence was there.

More often than not, the times that have shaken me to the core have been the moments in stillness when, in the eyes of another, I am startled by the image of Jesus staring right back at me.

That afternoon as the sun shone around us, I knew I was being given another gift. It would be this great reversal, where those who were supposedly in need of education would teach me in minutes what would take lifetimes elsewhere. We were being turned right on our heads! Little hands reached for mine. Laughter contagiously bellowed through the crowd around us, and we were immersed in childlike wonder.

Somehow, this jolt in us feels the pressure to perform, to save the world, to become the rescuer, to bring justice, and to "fix" the hellish realities of war, famine, disease, needs, and death around us. What we would learn was that the Rescuer had already come. We weren't the "great white" answer to the human crisis. Often, there were times when we didn't have a clue what we were doing!

I thought that I was supposed to give my life to "save the world." What these little hands would shake me back to life with was the truth that the world was already saved by the One who became a suffering servant. We didn't need to be the "women of power for the hour." All we were asked to do was to be as little children. Yielded, trusting, and willing—excited to be with the One who loves. It really wasn't about what we could do anyway. It was the fact that He would invite us to enjoy the ride with Him.

We are not called to be mothers and fathers to the poor. We aren't even to take the burdens of rescuing the afflicted. That's not our job. Our job is simple. We ask the Rescuer Himself to come, and He takes our little hands in His. Together, we watch as God becomes what only He can be—the One to save everyone, including ourselves!

We are invited to be sisters and brothers to those who are marginalized. In sitting with them, we join them as the overlooked, the downcast, the exiled, the forgotten, the messed up. Together, our cries reach a Father who is so very good at being Himself. One who so majestically fuses with us as a friend of sinners, a companion to those who are pushed out of the inner circles of society.

The road through Tanzania had just begun. Our time in Likamba would prove pivotal in what we would find ahead. As in many places throughout Africa, the children would pave the way to seeing more of this upside-down Kingdom in our midst.

Poverty of Spirit

Kneeling in the small village church, the cement under my knees was stamping my legs like molds from the floor's cracks and imperfections. Can you take a stab at what Randi was doing? Yes, you guessed it. There she was on the floor in a heavy haze. She has a daring love for Jesus that makes her run to wherever He is. I call it being a spiritual lush. She calls it hunger. So there I was on the concrete trying to figure out what in the world to do, while Randi was off somewhere vacationing with Jesus!

Widows and children filled the small village church. I can remember the deep blues and reds of the Maasai wraps dragging the floor from the women's skirts and the sweat pouring off our faces from the heat that swarmed the air around us.

Raw worship had become home. It was as if in each place we found ourselves opening our hearts together in intimate worship made us family. Each of us had needs. Some were more hidden than others. Our stories were so different from one another. We came from different cultures, had different backgrounds. Yet spiritual neediness was our common ground. It was the glue that held us together. It was what drew us together in the first place.

There are no words to fully describe a widow who desperately cries out for Jesus to be near her and to meet her like no one else could. How do you describe the awareness that happens when Heaven's presence is so thick that even the children are face-first, stuck on the concrete or dirt right next to you? Where's the logic in that? Where's the theological premise? Maybe it's time we identify it. I'd like to call it embodied Love.

A Dancing Tribe

Women in the third world amaze me. There is wisdom and strength coupled with an innocent joy emanating from within them. I look into their eyes and it is as if they know a secret that I do not know. It's almost an invitation into their reality and their experiences with Jesus that my background couldn't grasp without their help. It is an eyeful of intrigue. That gaze makes me want to sit and learn at their feet. Why had I gone after Jesus in the most institutionalized places—in schools and formulas only—when all along, my teachers were an ocean away waiting to give what they had freely?

As we were preparing to leave, Elirehema rounded up the entire village, young and old, for a "family" picture. I have never in my life seen smiles that large. I felt like a photographer on speed! I was rushing back and forth attempting to smash everyone into the lens' view. Randi and I pushed up against our new friends so tightly that we could feel each other's lungs expand to breathe.

I remember leaving with a heavy heart and wanting desperately to stay. The women began dancing. I had camped with a Maasai tribe when I was 18 in Tanzania for a time. Their rhythmic, wild dancing is a love language, an expression taught from the cradle, and unlike any other cultural movement I have ever experienced.

They asked us to join in on their dance. There we were—all one tribe. With brightly colored beaded collars around our neck, we mimicked as best as we could. I can still hear that laughter and music streaming through the air. As we were going away, the music would fade, but would continue lingering in our memories as yet another lesson on the margins of a world we never before knew existed.

The Shack

When we set out from Mozambique, we wondered if we would even have a place to sleep in each land that we would go. We set out with one point of contact, and the rest came through divine appointment. I remember thinking of all possible options before we left. We had no clue of what we would encounter, who we would meet, where we would sleep, what we would eat, or what we would wear. All I really cared about was having enough wet-wipes to do a mock wash-up every now and then!

The little wooden shack on the side of the road appeared to us as an oasis. In the beginning, I think we were hoping that out of the blue, banana plants would sprout out of nowhere with luscious fruits to feed us. We wished the land of "milk and honey" that originated in biblical accounts surrounded our newfound refuge. No such luck this day.

Randi counted the few shillings we had left.[3] I looked down in the small shack and saw a packet of spaghetti-type noodles and a little garlic. Without another word, it was settled. For the entire time in central and northern Tanzania, plain spaghetti and garlic would be our diet. I'm still convinced we could market the idea. This was in our minds—turbo-luxurious missionary fuel. We were thrilled! Though, thinking about it, I wonder how thrilled those in the wake of our audacious breath were!

Leaving the shack with prizes in hand, we continued on to the next point in our journey. With our packs on our backs we set off walking toward Moshi, a city on our next stop. There, we would meet a group of people at the foot of Mount Kilimanjaro.

At the Foot of Mt. Kili

Glorious and Josephine[4] were the leaders of an amazing children's home in Moshi, Tanzania, called The New Life Foundation. Our first night together was full of gut-busting stories. Over dinner, Glorious chimed in unannounced to let us in on how everyday life had changed for them as they followed the promises of God in their lives. His stories were filled with testimonies of demons being cast out and healings taking place on an everyday basis. In the retelling of these miracles, I couldn't help but laugh. He has this way of making the most complicated situations in our minds simple. There is this honesty of heart that provokes me to want what they have. His stories embrace no presumption. They are what they are—truth, raw, and untainted.

Naked truth is what we found in our time at the base of Mt. Kili. We were lost in our muse—inspiration for how life could look when we followed Jesus wherever He went—as we met a few hundred children the next morning. The New Life Foundation had built children's centers and a school. That morning, as the fog lifted over the mountain's peak beyond us, a haze descended on us down below.

The staff had gathered to meet with us early before school began. As we prayed for each teacher, the room began to take on a familiar hue—a partially visible and tangible cloud of God's presence.

The only common ground between all of these places we were visiting was spiritual hunger. We lingered there that morning, soaking in Jesus' presence, not caring about the list of "musts" that the day held. The room was filled with such weightiness that, as the bells rang for class, there we all were, learning what it meant to simply *be*.

Become What You See

Already, Randi and I were living with people who had nothing materially to speak of and yet possessed all things important to Heaven's economy. Looking back, we know that they were sent to rescue us. Under the shade tree in the days to follow, we would meet with those children. We would learn to imitate them. Life wasn't complicated anymore. Flashes of children crying out for Heaven to mingle with the earth in the dirt under the tree still flood my memory.

To hear His voice, see His face, and feel His touch—encounter is the entryway to becoming like Jesus. Children imitate their parents because of time spent in their presence. They become the reflection that they see in their parents' eyes.

Still, as I crashed into another split second when time seemed to pause, I wondered, "What do I really have to give? Are we changing anything around us? What will we leave behind?"

Heaven's Fingerprint

In the wake of my questions, there was one all-encompassing answer—one touch from Jesus. A life interrupted by Heaven's fingerprint—the transfer of Heaven's reality to ours. What do we really have to give? What matters in the end when eternity stares you in the face?

Exactly what happens in the wreckage of this collision between the natural and the spirit? It is much more than supernatural jargon. It's more than what we've accumulated, learned, or become. More than what we've stored up, worked up, or cooked up.

All I know is that I have this one life, these few breaths. What do I have to give? I can't "fix" people. I can only give what I have. A touch. That very same touch that interrupted my life and sent me on a path beyond my capabilities. This nugget of truth is so immensely opposite to what we have been told. What if this was for all of us? What if this was for the weak, the poor, the too young, and the too old? What would we do? Moreover, what could we do together?

Think about it. The times that shatter our paradigms are those moments that break us free from where we are and awaken us to the reality of what has been just out of reach before. One touch, one transfer from God's heart to ours—that's what love looks like!

The Dream

While in Moshi, I had a dream. I saw a map of Africa with Uganda highlighted as if with a marker. That's it. No heavenly appearance. No angel. Not even any directions. (Which all Heaven and earth knows I would need!)

Randi and I compared journals the next day and were baffled by the striking similarities on both of our pages. Uganda was where we were setting out for. Where would we stay? How would we get there? Wait a minute, what would we even do?

There was no answer. Just a marker-colored map highlighted in my mind.

I wish I could tell you that we were full of faith that could move mountains and *yadee da, blah blah blah.* The truth is, we questioned everything! Thankfully, our answer would come sooner than we could conceive.

As night fell that same day after the dream, Pastor Glorious came to speak to us. I can still see the grin on his face. The look of joy and mischievous knowledge, as if he knew something we didn't know.

"Girls, God wants you to go to Uganda. And we want to send you." We nearly keeled over. Randi laughed. I cried. There it was again. This joyous chaos that seemed to whip around while holding on with both hands to Glorious' coattails wherever he went.

We couldn't believe it. We heard a direction from God. We said "yes," and He stepped into our reality to do what He wanted in the first place. This *really* was happening before our eyes. And you know something else? We wouldn't just get to Uganda. We would fly.

On this next episode of *My Life as a Homeless Globe Traveler,* a tide would turn that would change our direction westward. I haven't even begun to scratch the surface of the stories that we left Tanzania with. The faces and embraces still echo in our memory.

In our own time, we were feeling the first signs of life that made our hearts jump with rhythm in the times when Heaven's presence would back us up with the weight that it carried. It was a living, breathing reality of God in us and in the world around us. It was during these beginning steps that we began to view our lives from Heaven to earth, not the other way around. This quest was much bigger than ourselves. It was much more than we could direct and create on our own.

Can You Hear the Beat?

That night, we could hear the drums of East Africa playing a cadence that would push through the winds of the villages around us. Our journey had just begun.

I am hoping that at this point you are beginning to feel this heartbeat within your own spirit. This pitter-patter was a constant reminder that life was being shaped within us. Mary would feel these movements bringing her new life, hope, freshness, maturity, and growth each morning as she would awake. Each day would bring a fresh encounter.

Heaven's heartbeat ripples through time in the most obscure places in our lives. If we listen, we can hear the sound. It is the sound of a dream taking shape and a promise that could only come from outside of ourselves.

As with Mary, we can do nothing to cause this miracle of life to take place. What's asked of us is to watch and wait each step of the journey as Jesus gives us a sneak peek into a movement that would shatter the minds of all around us. A movement that we are each invited to enter into—where God joins Himself with us.

This heartbeat is one of life and power. It is the Spirit's roar that all tribes, in every deep part of the earth and in every time that was, is, and will be, will carry in beautiful unison and harmony. It is the rhythm that will usher in Jesus' return again. What are we invited to do in response?

Just dance.

Endnotes

1. Lesley-Anne Leighton, director, Holy Given International School of Missions, www.holygiven.org.

2. *Dada* means "sister" in Kiswahili.

3. Shillings are the currency of Tanzania.

4.Glorious and Josephine Shoo, directors, The New Life Foundation, www.ministrytochildren.org.

Chapter 4

Jesus in the Dirt

We cannot help speaking about what we have seen and heard
(Acts 4:20 NIV).

Before I set out on this road, I thought that miracles were set aside for the "superheroes" of faith. They couldn't be for people like me. I didn't have the qualifications. And I certainly didn't have any superpowers. I couldn't see through walls with X-ray vision. I didn't possess superhuman strength. I didn't even have a bodacious costume. I was super-weak! I wasn't even sure that I believed miracles were authentic. The supernatural was—in my mind—associated with brightly colored lights, television cameras, and gold dust. Why? It had no relevance in my closed-in life. My framework was based on a stereotype and indirect experience.

I wondered, though, what would happen if we tore out the carpet, ripped out the colored lights and electricity, shut down our videocameras, and just asked Jesus to show up? Did God need a gift basket, red carpet, or five-star accommodations? It was in those questions that my eyes would be opened up to a whole new world. A place crying out in utter need for a God who could quench our thirst. No packaging required. No assembly necessary. And get this—it was free of charge!

We lunged into an awakening of Jesus in the dirt—dusty feet and all—beckoning us into a muddy baptism of endless proportions. A life full of wonder and adventure. A dive into love so upside down that it puts us on our heads.

Challenges

I looked down at our measly belongings already tattered and stretched out beyond recognition. Stuffing them again into our small backpacks, I peered out the windowpane one last time. The thick white fog rising up as from somewhere otherworldly covered the green East African ground that morning.

The elfin plane carried at most seven people. These were the flashes in time where I would give anything for a video crew! Sometimes, words are so very inadequate in comparison to the unbelievable happenings that take place before our eyes. Even if I were able to give them full justice, you probably wouldn't believe me.

As the plane took off over Tanzania's western border, it happened. Randi had this reflection in her eyes of utter panic. At this point, you might be expecting something dramatic. "Maybe the wing breaks off," you ponder. A crash? All wrong.

Randi stared intently down at her feet. Her pathetic little flip-flops were broken beyond repair. To those of you reading this thinking, "What's the big deal?"—let me bring you down to our level. When the only worldly goods you have to your name are stuffed sparingly into a backpack, a pair of shoes becomes like gold!

The road we were now on did not allow for bare feet. We would be entering the busy city streets of Kampala, Uganda, in less than 30 minutes' time. I offered Randi one of my sandals so that we would both have one bare foot. We didn't have money for a new pair of shoes. We didn't even know our way around Kampala. The risk of needles or broken glass was too high for us to chance it.

A few foreign women beside us, obviously on safari vacations, chimed in on our frantic brainstorming session. "I'd be happy to lend you a pair of my shoes," said one of the women. "I brought over five pairs just in case. You never know, do you?" I smiled as if trying to pretend that I knew where she was coming from.

A sigh of relief hit us like a cool mist. As the woman reached in her oversized bag, she added, "I'll give you the address of my hotel, and you can bring them back to me tomorrow."

My face went blank. That kind of masked stare where one unbelievable glare says it all. Remember that I laugh when I am nervous? Well, turns out, I also laugh when I am in shock. So there I am, giggling in sarcastic unbelief while Randi sinks back into her seat in emotional exhaustion. We were back to square one!

A Miracle on the Street

The swirling humid air seemed to wrap us in a cocoon of soaring temperatures. An orange-red dust blew through the streets and side paths. Carts pulled by thin, overworked men coasted by us at a generous speed. I looked and saw a woman carrying a load of bananas on her small head. On her back was a bundle of a baby, his head bobbing in the rhythm of her shuffling walk. I looked and could see sweat pouring from both of their tired brows.

Four traffic lanes were "ad hocked" into six or more. Horns and sirens were our welcoming ambiance. Thirsty, we made our way to a small store for water. I could hear the skidding sound of Randi's flip-flop as she strived to hold together the broken pieces of her shoes with her toes. Randi was a trooper; but this couldn't go on forever. We needed a miracle.

Randi prayed achingly aloud, "God, please help us!"

A few blocks down, we stopped to clear our lungs of the cloud of dust that encapsulated the air we breathed. Somehow, in the middle of the chaos around us, we found ourselves in silence, if only for a minute.

Randi's eyes had another reflection in them this time. It was a new message to give without any words. Her eyes were beaming with amazement. She pointed at her new discovery.

As I glanced down in contempt, I saw it—a safety pin. Not just a typical safety pin. A large, jumbo-sized safety pin! Many people would rather hear about food multiplying instead of mere childish miracles in the overcrowded streets of Uganda. To many, it would not be a big deal. For us, it was more than a big deal. God was with us!

God had answered our prayers. Randi managed to maneuver the pin through one end of her shoe to the other. Problem solved. Office supplies do not just appear in Africa. If you've been anywhere in the continent, you would share in this ecstatic realization. That one little miracle gave us more expectancy than all of the physical healing we had seen thus far.

There is something about knowing that all of Heaven is backing you up—covering you—that causes you to grin in the comfort of knowing you are secure. The knowing that says, "You are not alone." The opening of our eyes to see that Jesus will find His way within the most obscure parts of our lives, one breath at a time.

Just a Small-Town Girl

By nature I am a small-town country girl. Makeup, country music, and hair spray have always been my dearest of companions. Ask anyone who knows me. They are convinced that, instead of coal miner's lung, I'll develop hair spray lung should my habit continue!

I grew up on country greats and openly professed at the age of five that I was going to be the next Reba McEntire. (OK, truth be told, I still secretly do!) Between visions of the *Grand Ole Opry* stage, my diaper bag and life-like baby doll for "Mommy training," and my genuine *Wizard of Oz* ruby-red slippers, I had my life planned out. It's true!

I love bubble baths and spa days. Turns out, I would get a mud bath in a way I never before expected. So you can imagine the upside-down nature that my life has taken. How does a girl like me end up in the middle of the dirt in Africa's heart? Your guess is as good as mine. All I know is this—one touch, one look, one moment turned my life inside out. And there was no turning back. Something along the road kept me and has kept me ever since.

So there we were—two love-struck nomads of sorts, backpacks on with eyefuls of wonder at the expectancy of living life in the most unnatural, unpermissible of ways. We didn't need a strategy, a business plan, or a creative marketing agenda to persuade the laughter of Heaven to come. We didn't need programs or fundraising campaigns. No. All we needed was Him and the willingness to give all of ourselves.

My times in nearly two dozen countries have shattered my theological senses. In the wake of those cataclysmic explosions, the smallest and most miniscule of substance remained. Through the smoke, debris, and ashes, a small hand gripped onto faith.

It was this minute belief that it really wasn't about *me* anyway. It was a tangible expectancy that we would be a part of something bigger than ourselves. This expedition was bigger than those who comprised it. This movement was living and breathing. It was going somewhere. I knew this because I knew what it felt like to be a part of something that was really going nowhere at all.

Some liken that reality to expansion. I call it liberation. What was the point of all of these steps? All of these questions and risks? We wanted to see God. We really did.

We were together being wooed by a Love that gave itself for its enemy. The fulcrum of this entire odyssey was found on the margins, on the outskirts of society and commercial faith and practice. That was where we would find Him, already in the midst of nobodies like ourselves. All sharing one heart combined—spiritual hunger.

Victoria's Shore

Escaping the frantic streets of Kampala, we retreated to Lake Victoria's shore. Peace, Fred, and their son, Howard, greeted us. We were connected with this new family through a chance meeting with a man in Arusha, Tanzania. Peace is one of those women who make the world a fun place to live in. She has this sense of humor that sets people free from their inhibitions and openly states that she makes the best *matoke*[1] in all of East Africa!

I walked outside to the deck and peered out as night fell on Victoria's shore. In the distance, the shrieks and squeals of children playing hand ball with an old jerry can—a plastic jug we used to store water—made their way to my ears.

That night I wondered, "Why Uganda? Why now? Why us?"

This much I knew of love so far. It always came in packages I didn't expect. Sometimes, there was no package at all. No glitz or sparkle to add mystery to what would be underneath. It was just raw love. Messy love. Risky love. And yes, it was chaotic love.

I wanted to know why I was here. Were we really on the right track? There's something about being in an utterly foreign place that provokes this need in us of being known. I needed to know His eyes were on me still.

This much we both knew—we were thirsty. Not simply parched. We were desperate and more dependent than we had ever in our lives known. I lay down on the deck beneath me as night crept closer to my feet, the pink, yellow, and purple toned sunset rippling in the air above me.

"I need You, Jesus."

Tattooed by Heaven

A few minutes went by and nothing was happening. I felt alone. In my frustration, I determined to just get up and go to sleep. As I pressed myself against my hands, I had no luck. I tried again, thinking I must really need to work on my upper body strength. No matter how hard I tried, it didn't work. I was stuck. I felt like someone was draping a heavy blanket of heat over my back. The sounds of birds near the water began to fade. My heart was pounding in an increased rhythm. What was happening? I still don't know what to call it.

With my face pressed against the stone beneath me, a deafening sound enveloped me. How do you put into words the happening that takes place when your heart hears more than your ears?

As a weighty presence pressed tenderly on my back, tears came like a flood from within me. I wept tears of sadness, fear, joy, and burden—all of these in one. I wept rivers of tears filled with questions of trust that I carried. I was overwhelmed. Could I really trust Him with everything?

Not far away, I could hear the sounds of riots and chaos in the streets around us. There had already been deaths in the city from fighting that day. This wasn't a mere adventure story. I wasn't a fictional comic book character. This was real life with real consequences.

My life wasn't about safety. Our young "immortality complex" was thrown out the window a long time ago. We knew that we were not simply young and immortal. In fact, we were learning just how fragile our lives were becoming. This epic of ours was true life. Things didn't go the way they did in the movies or cartoon enactments. The characters aren't always saved in the end. The roadrunner in ACME productions might have always escaped death and left danger unscathed. But this wasn't television. It wasn't some romantic fairy tale. This was real life! It was my little, fragile, I-get-one-chance existence.

As tears continued to flow, I felt His hand on my back. It instantly brought me back to stepping onto the dirt in Africa for the first time a few years before. In times of joy and times of danger, I would feel that hand as if someone were actually there. It always reminded me that I wasn't alone.

Waves of understanding washed over me as night fell. He didn't expect me to become someone famous or change a nation. He just asked me to trust. Sometimes that seemed more difficult than any other request.

How long had I been there? I have no idea. An hour? Three? All I know is that there was more He wanted to show me. When I couldn't trust on my own, He would pour trust out freely upon me.

I looked and before me I saw Jesus walking near. I could see what looked like a large nail or stake in His hands. Jesus came to where I was and began marking me with the nail in His hands, which was inked in deep red. He began writing on me the words, "The Lord's." He did not write in small letters but in bold ones. He did not merely tattoo my forehead and wrists, but I was covered from head to toe with His seal. I was completely covered. So much so that I was not able to cover the marks—nor was I able to remove the ink of the words. I couldn't hide anymore. These marks were non-erasable, permanent. All of eternity would read them as sure and true.

> But for now, dear servant Jacob, listen—yes, you, Israel, My personal choice. God who made you has something to say to you; the God who formed you in the womb wants to help you. Don't be afraid, dear servant Jacob, Jeshurun, the one I chose.

> *For I will pour water on the thirsty ground and send streams*
> *coursing through the parched earth. I will pour My Spirit into*
> *your descendants and My blessing on your children. They shall*
> *sprout like grass on the prairie, like willows alongside creeks.*
> *This one will say, "I am God's," and another will go by the*
> *name Jacob; that one will write on his hand "God's property"—*
> *and be proud to be called Israel* (Isaiah 44:1-5).

He said that my life was no longer my own. He said His promises for me were finished and sealed. He said, "No looking back. You are Mine."

I looked and I saw Jesus laying down the nail He had used to mark me with. I saw His hands worn and worked. Not the hands of a fine prince. No, they were the hands of a workingman, a servant. And do you know what He did? He bent down to my level. He got low just for me!

I saw Him again face to face. Those unforgettable eyes filled with hunger and fullness, sorrow and joy. Eyes filled with oceans of swirling color and love all at one glance. Eyes that spoke more words than all of human language could possess.

I saw His face stained in blood-filled tears. This was my Jesus. He, too, knew what it meant to be weak and tired. The good, the bad, and the awful—He knew it all. One more look in His eyes changed everything. Looking into His eyes caused the environment around me to look dull and old. The screams from the riots were drowned out by the sound of timelessness. How do you write that in mortal language?

As I looked into Love's eyes, I saw hunger. Though in this case His hunger had a name. It was mine.

Muddy Miracles

Following the dirt roads near Kampala the next day, we made our way to a village church. The room looked more like a mud pit than a sanctuary. Heavy rains had brought a flood in the unsheltered area. I looked down at my feet as a cockroach nonchalantly skipped across my toes as if it had just hailed a taxicab. By this point, I didn't even flinch. Be it apathy or adaptability, I don't know.

I scanned the large area held up by little more than some sheet metal and rope. Plastic chairs with Coca-Cola logos were sporadically squeezed between splintery wooden benches. The freshly created mud was makeshift quicksand as it sunk the seats into the depths below.

We didn't have a bag of tricks. We were lucky to have anything at all in our bags in the first place. What was God going to do? This nervous sensation of invisible "butterflies" crammed my stomach in expectancy.

As music began to flow through the air, a wind began to blow through the place with a force that shook the metal encasing all of us from the surrounding rain. Tattered fabrics of pink and green danced from the small wooden twig Cross above us. What was happening? Gazing back, I'm still not sure that we fully know.

A deep, heavy sound began to waft through the air around us in harmonic unison. In the mud, I lifted my head to get a look at its origin. Scanning the sea of faces, I saw beauty in a way I had never before known.

A little boy on top of his knees, obviously caught up somewhere beyond me, captivated my attention. His face was one of innocence and wisdom all at one glimpse. I watched as tears streamed down his tiny cheeks. There is a big difference between tears of hunger and tears of being overwhelmed by the answer to that longing.

The love that was being poured out drowned out all my thoughts. My head was complete mush as a man handed me a microphone attached to a slithering green and orange cord. There it was—this realization that nothing mattered but His presence with us. The smells of smoke and sounds of destruction from the riots around us all dimmed in comparison to the river that was washing over us like waterfalls of liquid mercy. "Jesus, we need Your presence."

Another Mary knew this well. Pouring out everything she had only to be filled up again from head to toe, she laid everything at His feet—all that she was. With her long, dirt-filled hair, she wiped His feet in the oil of offering.

The fragrance that filled the room would become familiar as Mary could trace His steps in the aroma that followed. She was like us. Wanting nothing else but to follow Him wherever He went.

The reality of this moment shocked me. Literally! The microphone, now drenched in the mud, was sending jolting and increasing shock waves through me at each breath. We had no invitation to give. He had already sounded a clear call with arms wide open. We simply wanted to join into what He was already doing.

Hundreds swarmed the front with little regard of the mud entrenching them. Our four short arms couldn't reach all of them for prayer. But it didn't matter. I watched frail, fragile bodies drop to the ground, overwhelmed by a touch that only Heaven could give.

St. Francis of Assisi once said, "Preach the gospel and, if necessary, use words." Why were we here? We were there to join in hunger.

The Mud Man

Out of the corner of my eye, the most unusual of paradoxes caught my stare. There in the mud face-first was a regal man, suit and all. Now, let me bring you up to speed. We were in the middle of nowhere. There were no buildings and certainly no one rich enough to possess anything but hand-me-down rags. Why would a suited man be with us? More than that, why would he let his riches fall and sink into the mud?

Crawling over, Randi and I began to lay our hands on him and pray. Tears washed the ground beneath him, which was completely out of context with his rough and untouchable exterior.

What was happening? As mud became muddier, buckets of healing doused him with fluidity. He was being baptized in love. Knowing Jesus wasn't about going to church at all. It was about encountering Him for who He is, delving into His heart, and never leaving.

What began as an insane morning continued to shatter our minds in the minutes that would follow. With the help of a few other men, the man was able to at least get to his knees. People were obviously not going anywhere soon. And with that we decided to extend our time and linger as long as God would remain.

I hobbled out to the little shack beside us for a drink of water. In the sunlight that was now beaming down after the rain, I saw a rainbow. As I looked, there was none other than the "mud man" running out toward us.

In between shallow breaths, he began to recount encountering God's presence in a way he had never before experienced. "He's real!" he shouted with eyes so big, you would have thought he had witnessed a UFO!

I wanted to know how a man of his stature out of nowhere found his way to the bush with us. His story amazed us. "I was heading to my office this morning, and a voice told me to come to this village."

Turns out, the man was an esteemed member of both the government of South Africa and the parliament of Uganda. He was hungry for more, he told us. "Please come to Parliament!" he yelled with no less energy than when he began.

"There are others there. Come and pray for us so that my friends get this, too!"

The look in my eyes triggered an even more extreme reaction in Randi's. We knew this would happen. As his words pierced our ears, memories were hurled back to us in our conjoined stares.

They came through a very unexpected source. Words rushed back from a man we had met in passing in Tanzania. He wanted to pray for us. You know us by now. We could use all the prayers we could get! We accepted as if he were offering us gold.

His words rang through our ears. *"You will be put before governments soon. Walk through those doors. Set before leaders, you will speak truth and hope. Give what you have. The doors are opening soon."*

Here's a thought. When you are called to carry God in the earth, who do you turn to? Are there any among you who will understand? Any who will help you with the load? Or are we simply thrown into a life of mystical hermitage, of spiritual celibacy?

God's universal game plan has always been in a team format. Each of us carries different gifts, weaknesses, and quirks. The comforting part is that we never have to go through life alone. We were meant for one another, to share life together.

Mary's Song

Groggy under the stupor of a foggy dream, she lifted her head from her pillow. Stretching, the awareness of the night before hit her with a rush of remembrance.

Was it all a dream? And how in the world would she articulate the changes that would soon be taking place? How long could she wear over-sized clothes to hide what was growing within her? She couldn't hide. This was something the world would see with open eyes.

"I know that this favor is such a gift. But this gift could get me into so much trouble," Mary thought. "Is there anyone out there who will actually hear me? Believe me? Linger with me in this waiting?" She wondered, "Will I carry this promise alone?"

Mary knew only one person who might still welcome her in the midst of this insane journey. She raced to put on her dress, slipped on her sandals, and flew out the door, stopping only to brush her mother and father with a good-bye kiss.

Being overshadowed by Heaven was the most intense experience of this young woman's life. Where would she turn in the wake of its aftermath?

Mary ran, and when she did she did not stop. She ran through the hills. Some of them were rocky and even more were slippery. There was no other way. No short cut or back road that would get her there more quickly. No, she would have to take this path given to her. How long was this part of her journey? Mary would have to travel one hundred miles from Nazareth to the neighborhood of Maon. How long would that have taken?

Exhausted, she made it to the door. Bursting in, she cried, "Elizabeth!" Deep breaths made her sentences more of a staccato musical piece than a proper greeting.

"Elizabeth" was all she could get out. As she struggled to catch her breath, Elizabeth was nearly knocked over.

Elizabeth was pregnant, too. She had been carrying one who would also crash the world scene with audacious exile and piercing words. He would be a forerunner who would make way for Mary's promise.

Mary would not be alone.

The baby recognized the remains of Mary's encounter and leaped within Elizabeth. This heartbeat was now a raging gong of sorts. As both mothers saw what was happening, they looked at one another in wonder and amazement.

Picture Elizabeth knocked to the floor. In the midst of this visit, she was being filled with the Holy Spirit right there in the dirt. Neither of them had a framework for this. It was most certainly not temple-worthy conduct.

Yet they waited.

Both women would learn what it meant to carry a movement of Heaven to earth. Elizabeth, too, would catch that same cry of, "Yes!" Like Mary, she was invited into a new movement of God hitting the world scene. She was asked to participate—to join the team!

Mary found another who would stand by her as the days went by. When the unknown became known, they would be in the movement together. Her cousin did not need explanation from the night before.

"Thank God!" Mary thought. There was no possible way to communicate it anyway.

Without as much as an inkling of what had happened, Elizabeth sang words that would linger within Mary's memory for the rest of her life.

"You are blessed, little one. You believe even when others don't. You take the good and the bad. You've said, 'yes.' Heaven will do the rest."

In the shock that followed in the shadow of Elizabeth's words, what would they do? Simply sing. And they would sing with all their might. That song of vision would carry through the wind that morning to the corners of the earth. It is the same song that you and I are given today. It is a song of joy and hope—an anthem of freedom that rises above the ashes of war. When the curtain is drawn, will we sing?

Just sing.

God is sending new anthems throughout the earth in our day. They are anthems that point to the One who we will give up everything for. Songs of deep worship that shake the earth with Heaven's presence with us. Will you open your mouth and sing?

When God blows a big breath of hope our way, it startles us enough to forget, if even for a minute, about the questions and fear in carrying our promise. Most of us initially have no words to describe what has been placed inside of us anyway. Still, there is this knowing that draws us on. This eagerness that wants to so boldly run and jump into the deep of being used to shower God around us in the earth.

In places of obscurity, having others who share a similar heartbeat lightens our load as we realize more and more that we simply cannot do it alone. Mary had been given an incomprehensible gift and dream. It didn't originate with her. No, it was much too large. Promises are given. Along the road, as we carry them in expectation, we meet others on the same pilgrimage. Our heart becomes our compass. Our voices join with the melody of many who are sounding the same cry.

Barefoot in the Palace

Going to parliament in Uganda is like going to meet with the president of the United States in the White House. Apparently, it was a regal occasion. In our usual fashion, we would be busting through the iron doors straight from spending a day in a breathtaking village with muddy feet and all. Rushing through the city streets, I laughed. I could see our reflection in the eyes of those we passed on the streets. There we were— African *katangas* wrapped around our waists, nail beds filled with dust even after our painstaking attempt at wiping them clean, and windblown hair. Randi's makeshift sandal made me smile. I wondered what we were getting ourselves into but figured it would be something we would never in a million lifetimes forget.

The debris of rocks and sand caked our trusty flip-flops as we walked up to the security screening. Officials armed with machine guns and confused glares ushered us over to be scanned. They asked for our bags. We had none. There we were, going empty-handed into the House of Parliament of Uganda. As we walked up to the large stairs, a flash from the old *Rocky Balboa* movie danced through my mind. However, I resisted the urge to run to the top and shout "Adrian" at the top of my lungs. (Even though it would have made for an amazing photographic memory and even better story to tell our future grandchildren!)

Exquisite cars brushed by us, filled with men covered in crisp lined suits. As they stepped up to the doors with us, I looked down at our feet.

In one view, shoes so shiny that you could see your reflection within them. On the other side, bare feet with the slight evidence of a thin sole underneath. We were so unbelievably unprepared.

As we were thrust into the large banquet room, immediately a woman came up to us as if in an urgent haste. "The ceremony is beginning. Follow me." What ceremony? I looked at Randi in search of an answer. Nothing. "This should be one for the record books," I thought.

A Poor Man's Robe

As I sat there immersed in conversation about international politics and issues that spanned leaders from many countries, I felt awkward sitting in my comfortable chair presenting myself in this way. There was something in me that felt I needed to "look the part," "be something," and "represent." An official suddenly highlighted us. Introducing us as his special guests, he asked us to stand.

Looking around the room, extravagant dresses filled with colors across the rainbow caught my eye. There were suits lined in silk and, right in front of me, a crystal clear pitcher of sparkling blue water. I stared out the window and saw an entirely different world.

Sitting there in deep contemplation, I saw barefooted children playing just outside of the palace gates. I wondered what Jesus would look like if He were to sit next to me that afternoon.

Tears ran down my face as I saw a picture of Jesus, not sitting near me, but outside the palace gates with the children who were playing. He wasn't wearing a rich man's robe but one of a poor man. It wasn't shiny or colorful, but tattered, worn, dull, and brown. I watched Him take hold of the fence that separated us from the rest of the world. Looking into His deep eyes, I saw a smile stretch across His face as if beckoning me to join in with the fun that was out there to be had.

Jesus had chosen so long ago where He would dwell. He would be homeless, but would make His existence known on the margins—on the other side of the fence and tracks. His eyes were on the forgotten, the hurting, and the needy—even the misfits. And it was in those places of intense need that He would choose us as His own habitation.

Who did He spend His time with during His days on the earth? Who were His friends? Known as the "Friend of sinners," He joined the nobodies and the outcasts in all the messy realities of life. Where did He often heal? What people did He handpick to carry Heaven with Him? Who washed His feet? They were the unlovely, the unwanted, and the used.

He would take the unlovely and give them dignity and beauty. He would grab the unwanted and call them His own. He would pick up the used and make them brand-new. Where did He live? He resided in lives without selfish ambition and hidden agendas. Empty ones that gave Him room to possess everything they had.

Jesus would storm the palace with muddy feet that afternoon. As I snapped back to attention in the room, we were invited to pray for the leaders and for the nation of Uganda. Representatives from many nations including the West stood stiffly in their regal demeanor expecting a "nice" and brief time of prayer.

What would come next would shock even us. As we prayed, hunger filled the room. Women began to reject the pressure to be presentable, and together cried out for God's presence to overwhelm them and their people. Some joined in. Others looked on as shocked spectators. What happens when holy chaos sweeps the palace? Self-sufficiency is torn down. In its place is simple trust and dependence. Jesus didn't need a red carpet rolled out for Him. As we left the room, bodies still lined the floor, being touched by a true invasion from Heaven. Jesus would come even if there was just one who was willing. He found a few that day.

That night, Randi and I walked down to the water to pray. Feverish from an infection on my knee that had swollen to a size that made it hard to walk, I looked up at those unforgettable stars. The moonlit path was like a magnet that drew us. Sitting there on the edge, I remembered what God had shown me a few countries ago on the water in Mozambique. He promised to lead us. He knew the way. We had no clue. But we were here.

Stumbling back to our room, I took one last look at the moon. It was so incredibly massive. So close that it seemed within our reach. We were getting somewhere. It was a place deep within His heart.

A Shaking

I heard our guitar hit a frantic note as it was heaved through the air, landing on the other end of the room. At first, I thought I was dreaming. The room was shaking, and wind blew through the window in waves that nearly took my breath away. In a state of shock I screamed to Randi, "What's going on?"

She must have been sleeping as hard as a rock because the answer that followed still rings in my ears. (I also still use it to make fun of her, too!) "It's just the rain, Jess. Go back to bed." Then silence.

It was more than rain. Our beds were skidding across the cement floor. The mosquito nets were ripping in the air from the amount of force blasting from all sides. We were caught in the middle of an earthquake with a magnitude that Uganda had never before been introduced to. Aftershocks continued into the morning.

Now, I am an inland country girl. The closest thing to an earthquake I had ever experienced was a ride at the county fair. I thought we were going to die! In the meantime, Randi continued in blissful beauty sleep. This was another "first" for each of us to file into our memory. When I thought about it, I saw the temple and veil split in two after Jesus' death. It was Heaven's stamp of a new reign. A shaking that would change the earth forever—the culmination of Mary's cry in one glance.

That shaking would awaken a nation in Mary's day. That same shaking lingers within each of us. Waiting for one, just one, who will carry it to those around them and chance the ride.

Too Heavy to Carry Alone

Heaven hungers for us to enter in and carry part of its DNA to the world around us. This promise made before time began is a vow that could only come from outside of ourselves. This, too, is for you and me.

Have you heard the voice of God? Have you heard it internally or externally? It really doesn't matter how. What has He said to you? What has He put inside of you? Promised you? How will it come forth? It will come forth because of Love. That is His nature. It is who He is.

Have you ever wondered about your purpose and the promises of God over your life? Why did He choose us? Why did He pick you? What is His purpose for you? What is His purpose in choosing you? What does He see that we don't?

God wants you to understand that the destiny that He wants to place inside of your life is naturally impossible. You cannot create what God wants to birth through you.

We cannot do it on our own.

When God began whispering to me about what He would bring about in my life, I was completely overwhelmed and concerned. I had no grid to process the promise. What would it look like? What would it cost me? What would people think? How do I know this is true?

Mary didn't understand, either. Yet, in the midst of her gigantic questions—not to mention an actual angel running into her room—her answer remained. "Yes." We cannot produce or conjure up what God has promised us. We cannot create it, change it, or carry it alone.

When I set out on this path I was just a small-town girl who wanted to know what it meant to love. To love God and love people everywhere. Not a flippant love that lasts for seconds, but a love that consumes everything in its path. Not a love that makes me known and heroic. I was searching for a love that is breathing and powerful—a love that changes things.

God has always had a desire for family. He wanted to have a family and for His Son to have a Bride. Mary and Elizabeth would stand together, yes, as cousins in the natural. But they would become sisters and partners in the Spirit. When God breathes a promise over us and in us, He doesn't expect us to do it alone.

Yes, we need Him. We need His presence. Without it, we might as well throw in the towel. He gives us others around us who will carry Heaven with us together.

When the promise inside of Elizabeth encountered the promise within Mary, it leaped inside of her. You can feel that when you come across others who share in the promise. This is a pledge and a cry to call forth the promise in others.

As Mary gasped a greeting to Elizabeth and called her name, the promise within Elizabeth was called forth, called to attention, to hope and life. A new movement of God is already moving in the earth around us. Jump in and join.

A Trek Along the Nile

Randi's brother Nate flew into Uganda to join our team. Tattoos, dreadlocks, and gauged ears (earrings that stretched his earlobes), Nate was Heaven-sent. It felt like Christmas morning! Randi and I hadn't been with our families for Christmas the year before. This day made up for all of it. In Nate's clean, fresh bags were a couple new shirts, some new shoes, and best of all, makeup and candy! We had all we could ever ask for, right there in one handful. Sugar and lipstick—the stuff that makes the world go round!

The next morning, we set out on a road trip north to Uganda's border town of Arua with friends. It was a miracle in itself that we made it in the first place because none other than yours truly was behind the wheel. Nate's first peek into Africa's heart would be in Sudan, over 16 hours away.

With backpacks slung in the trunk and five people stuffed into the undersized car, we were on our way. You know, some days can be hard and full of chaos. There are days when I want to take my life back and just for once take a warm bubble bath. There are also days when all of Heaven just can't help but smile and roar with laughter at the beauty of a simple life and at the idiosyncrasies of its kids.

Nate's introduction into Africa was one of the most comical experiences I have ever witnessed from the outside. Western music in Africa is a bit dated. And by a bit dated, I mean that "new releases" came from the eighties at best. Driving along the road, our friends wanted to make us feel at home. "We have some music from America for you. We think you will like it." I was expecting some kind of techno genre but secretly crossing my fingers for one of country music's latest hits! "Please God, let it be Garth Brooks!"

To make us feel more at home, the music would not be at a gentle volume, but our friends would blare it full blast the entire five hours to Arua. In my expectancy, I hurried them. What would it be?

Suddenly a flashback from the movie *Titanic* ambushed my mind. Yes, you guessed it. Celine Dion in all her glory. I wanted to pass out, nearly purple from laughter-filled tears. Glancing in the rearview mirror, the look on Nate's face was priceless. He was terrified. This was his first immersion into a journey that would forever keep us on our toes. As the cassette tape flipped over to play her ancient album for the fifth consecutive time, I looked over at Randi mouthing the words, "If you can't beat'em, join'em."

So there we were, driving along through villages and black sand, singing at the top of our lungs, "my heart will go on," and *yadeeda*. This time, as I peered back in the mirror, there was Nate "interpretively dancing" sarcastically with self-abandon. Then the realization came. I was home. I had been beckoned into a place where inhibitions would flee and family would reign. God wasn't asking us to be "rock stars" of faith. He was asking us to be children, embracing each little nook and cranny of life and the world around us. Earth was our playground. He would come and spin with us each step of the way.

When Heaven Smiles

On a donut tire, we coasted into the dirt lot of the hostel in Arua. Our back tire had popped in one of the bazillion craters that covered the "roads" we had to take. Along the Nile River, we were stranded for a few hours while mending the problem. The current flowed with an intensity I had never before encountered. With the agonizing sounds of Celine Dion karaoke tracks tormenting and ringing in my ears, I looked around at the banana trees covering the small building around us.

That's when I heard her before I saw her. There were shrieks of joy, courage, and laughter all in one. Michele[2] had been on a journey as well. Going to Sudan with little more than a bag, she had created a place that was home for 50 children in a small village in southern Sudan. Hearing her greeting made something within me jump and rise up. I felt like I had met another who understood with me what this journey was like. She had been there, too.

In just a few hours, we would be on our way, crossing Uganda's northern border into Sudan. With our small green guitar that we had named "Norb," we began to worship together. Music filled the little cement room. Strumming the few chords I had learned, we asked Jesus to come right to where we were. Together, there was something in the air around us that just knew He would come. There was no question in our minds.

Heaven was crashing in with nothing more to welcome it than a few nobodies on a shared pilgrimage to find His face. A startling heaviness fell on my shoulders and there it went. The poor little green guitar was crashing to the floor, and myself along with it.

There on my face, Michele began to call out the promise within me as Mary had for Elizabeth.

"At your voice wells will be released. You are called to carry the glory. What you have seen in your heart, what you have seen in the Spirit, you will see with your eyes."

Face-first, shoved against the cold concrete, I saw Africans running to Jesus. Northern Africa and the Middle East set on fire by God's tangible presence. I heard the words, "Arabian Peninsula." Where or what was that? This wasn't a wave of a few, but thousands running in one heavy, combined motion toward Him. What happens when we yield ourselves to let Heaven overshadow earth? The promise we once believed was impossible looks us in the face, making itself known right in front of our eyes.

Somewhere within this process of birthing a promise—your promise—God wants to grow more love within your being. The finishing touches of a creation that could only find its genesis in Him.

Whether you have had an angel burst into your room or a gentle knowing within yourself, each one of us has been destined to be carriers of Heaven, to bring Jesus glory in the lives we encounter around us. Each one of us has a promise and a purpose. We cannot make it happen. We can say "yes," and in that "yes," dive into intimacy with Jesus beyond what we have ever imagined.

God is not just choosing the few "oddballs" who run throughout the earth. This is for us—for you and for me. Listen. Can you hear it? Heaven's cadence is searching for the nobodies, the weak, the unknown, the hidden, the exiled, and the broken. Are you one of them?

Mary wasn't called to carry Heaven alone. There would be others along the way who would walk together down a similar path. A road unpaved. What about you? What will you say? Will you say "yes"?

Endnotes

1. *Matoke* is an African dish of mashed plantains. It tastes like mashed potatoes.

2. Michele Perry is field ministry director of Iris Ministries Sudan and heads Converge International, www.changethewayyousee.org.

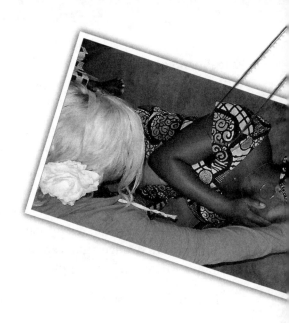

Chapter 5

For Love's Sake

> *"Blessed is the season which engages the whole world in a conspiracy of love."*
> —Hamilton Wright Mabie

Remember Mary's first night of shock when she was given a vision and message that would shatter the earth's ideas of a kingdom and a reign that had no end? It would first shake her to the core of her very being. Before her promise would ever reach the realm of humanity, before anyone would see it for what it truly was, Mary was given a choice. Why would she say "yes"?

We often look at Mary as a superhero. An untouchable, you might say. I tend to think that Mary was a commoner like us. She was an everyday person whom God just couldn't keep Himself from smiling over. We do know that she was a poor, small-town girl in Israel. She had no intention of a life different from the norm around her. In her everyday, ordinary life setting, something blew her ideological boxes to oblivion. Starting to look familiar?

Why would she endure pain and suffering? Why continue on when our promise becomes hard to carry? History doesn't tell us anything about Mary's first nine months or about her everyday reaction to the heavenly development inside of her. We aren't given a sneak peek into her conversation with her parents when she let them in on the news she had been given. What would that have looked like? Did she like being pregnant? Some women do. Or did she have swollen ankles and morning sickness that kept her face in a constant shade of green? Did she feel awkward? What was it like?

Heaven has always lived for love. God fashioned us for love. He left the glory for the dirt all for love. He is Love! He is asking the same for us. Why did Mary say "yes"? Was it out of obligation? Fear? Did she simply have nothing better to do? Or was she completely head over heels love-struck with one look into Eternity's eyes? Mary's cry was for Love's sake.

When we begin to say "yes," to give everything out of the place of knowing we are loved, people are touched with a power that transforms the lowly into princes and princesses. It is a love that reshapes orphans into sons and daughters. What would life turn into if we began living out of what God has done for us instead of what we can do for Him? Emptiness converges into overwhelming fullness—waves of hope that awaken us to who we really are and what has been given to us. God wants to participate with us. As we give up all that we are, He pours Himself in fullness into our empty lives.

Could Mary see the citadels in the dust around her? Could she see beyond what was in front of her? Could she see beyond the suffering? Was she able to look beyond the pain? Maybe. Or did she simply trust that she would be taken care of? We don't know. We do know that Mary continued on in the midst of danger and fear. She gave everything away for Love. She gave up her rights, her dreams, and all that she had planned.

Today there is a new movement making its way through the lowest ranks of the earth. What is taking place is not dependent upon us. This is a global happening. It spans nations. God is not just asking us to bridge Heaven and earth. He is searching the earth for those who will link themselves on the margins—those who will cross borders, nations, and boundaries, leaving behind our identity in anything other than who we are in Him and embracing our place as a global, borderless tribe.

Land Mines, Life, and Laughter

My head smashed into the ceiling of the Land Rover as we ramped off yet another crater in the dirt and rocky "road" headed to the Sudanese border. Michele, Randi, and I were crammed in the back between boxes of medicine and other supplies. Our giggles were so contagious that there was a constant background noise of laughter.

Our lives had been flipped upside down, and we were headed straight for a village that would ruin me for any other kind of life. Randi's words stuttered as the vibrations of the Land Rover's movement pounded her up and down, "Are you sure these are even roads?"

The rainy season had swamped the red dirt pathway ahead of us. I looked out the window, gazing at mountains and lush green vegetation around us. A journey of a few hours soon turned into ten hours. In the distance, we could see the barbed wire fencing at the border crossing. There it was—the line that separated us from yet another run-in with destiny.

Driving into the small dirt lot, a few bamboo sticks lined the home like a flimsy fortress of protection. Underneath the bamboo in the tiny holes that lined the fence, I could see them. There were one hundred small feet, dancing back and forth. Michele's new family made me marvel. When I looked at her life, I saw someone who had learned to go with the beautiful and the ugly and press on to her promise. She was seeing it birthed before her eyes. As I peered at the children, I would catch a glimpse of what lay ahead for me in the years to come.

Oil Lamps and Oil From Heaven

I opened my eyes as flashes of dancing flames within the lanterns nearby caught my gaze. The cold cement underneath me felt shocking yet relieving in the heat of the thick, smoldering summer night.

The small village of Yei was abundant in activity around us. Through the small opening in our cement room, the giggles of children being scurried off to bed filled the air like a midnight lullaby. Michele, Randi, Nate, myself, and a few others filled the small, ten-by-ten-foot room. Through the dimming lamplight, I watched Nate fall in a heap to the ground beneath him, overwhelmed by God's presence in a way that he later revealed he had never before experienced in his life.

I looked over to my left. Randi lay there weeping and laughing. Her voice was carrying far into the dark moonlit Sudanese expanse. Michele, in her usual demeanor, was stuck on the ground somewhere in the middle. There I was, caught somewhere between laughing at Randi's strange experience next to me and crying out for Jesus to make His home more in us that night. This was wild! I was shocked even in the middle of it. It was like we were caught in a whirlwind that wouldn't slow down. Again, all I can term it is holy chaos.

What happens when you get a room full of people who all carry Heaven inside of them? What takes place when you set those with radical promises from God close to one another? Lock them in a small cement and spider-filled room with nothing but a little lamplight and oil, and all Heaven breaks loose!

God reawakens us to our destiny and who we are through others who know what it's like to be on the journey with us. This is the place we are meant to dwell. It is a place of shared need with others who have said "yes" with us. Crawling throughout the room, we prayed for one another and began to call out the promises that we saw within in each other's lives.

Sometimes the road can be rough. Especially one that's completely un-paved! When God tells you a secret—that you will participate in a new move of God in the earth around you—things can get hectic. There are so many unknowns. So much that He can see that we just cannot. In the midst of the mud, though, there are others with a similar promise. We were not alone. And in the times when the road got messy and seemingly impossible to continue on, He showed up to remind us that this pilgrimage carried many others, all in a hidden movement together, and breathed new life over us once more.

When you are discouraged, find someone who carries a promise, too. With Mary, one connection with God changed the entire world. What is your promise? You may not be able to see it, but you can feel it within you. You carry His heartbeat. Listen to it. Follow where it leads. Find where He is and run there. The increasing cadence within awakens us to the urgency of the emergence of what is coming—the reality of our dream. The larger it gets, the more uncomfortable we feel, the closer we are drawing near to the birthing of what we have been told.

God wouldn't just be spending time with us. He would be reworking the road ahead. Yes, I made fun of Randi for this hilarious experience that she was caught in. But God was really working! In a vision, Randi saw three angels shoot arrows into the world. She saw us in Sudan and the angel thrust his arrow. It landed in Israel. She watched another arrow mark its spot in Germany and the last in North America. (Turns out that would be Randi's exact steps ahead, even as we separated for a brief interlude of time.)

Our next stop would be the Middle East. We will get back to this amaz-ing story in a minute. First, let me take you into the life of a little girl that showed me a reflection of myself one day at a time.

Talia's Story

Her face was a mirror into my own life. The longer I looked into her eyes, the more I saw of myself. She was fragile and strong all at the same time. Her eyes carried stories within them that I doubted anyone had ever been told before.

Her name meant grace, and that is what she would give to me. Talia was two, her small blue dress and orange flip-flops too large for her petite body. She looked over at me, staring as if sizing me up for quite a long time. Her uninterrupted stare caught my curiosity. Minutes seemed to turn to hours as I made a point to connect my eyes with hers every now and then as if playing a game of tag. Each connection we made, she would shuffle closer to test me even more.

By the second day, we had a routine. Talia would sneak up next to me and jump in my lap. I could see the sadness in her eyes. She never said a word. Never uttered a sound. But her eyes said what no words could express. And each day, for hours, she would sleep right on my chest, while I learned what no one else in the world could impart to me.

I knew her story well. Her father was gone. Life had been immensely tough on her family. It was especially grueling on her mother. Then one day, it was too much. Just like that, in mere minutes, Talia would be motherless. No explanation. No warning. There was just striking, sudden pain.

Michele had given her a home and a family. She was handed a chance to be loved and cared for. But Talia would have to learn to let herself be loved one day at a time. She would fight it. Yet, when she was too exhausted from struggling, she yielded herself to Love. She was given a new mother. But she would have to first learn to be a daughter. This was by far one of the hardest lessons to learn for one who had only a little under three years to define what the words *daughter, mother, family, safety,* and *love* meant in her world.

This new love would be upside down to all she had ever known, all she had experienced. Life had taught Talia in two short years that she wasn't worth sticking around for. Here, she was learning that no matter what she did, she would be delighted in. If she didn't speak, she would be loved. If she kicked, screamed, and bit, she was still in the affection of the family. She was loved and worth giving your life for, no matter if she believed it as truth or not.

In Talia's eyes, I could see myself. I could see a little girl who fights and kicks against my Father's attempt at radiant, uncensored love. One who finds it so incredibly mysterious that Heaven takes delight in me at every waking hour of the day. To know His eyes are on me, each step of the way.

Why do we fight love? What is there about us that shies away from being called beautiful and precious? When we know we're loved, nothing can abort the promises of God within us. No valley can cause the life that is within us to die. Nothing can stop the heartbeat of Heaven inside of us. Nothing.

Yes, a life given away for love will cost you. But it doesn't end in cost. It is blessed. There is a clear voice of God's heart of love to you and who you know you are. Because of that sound, in your best moments you are overwhelmed by it like it is water drowning you in the best way with the best delight full of promises that echo through your spirit. That is what is real.

Bush Rat Stew Theology

The lantern light was dimming and beads of sweat were running down my face. I was dizzy, my hands felt locked in place, and the room was spinning like a circus ride gone bad. The heat of the night was so incredibly intense that even the mosquitoes were nowhere to be found. In my fever-induced hallucinations, I drifted off to sleep.

The reality of my fifth case of malaria was an interesting addition to my time in Sudan. As the afternoon heat scorched the ground below it the next day, my fever was worse. The village we were now in was remote and had just been plagued with an outbreak of meningitis. I'll tell you more about this beautiful land in a bit, but let's get back to this not-so-gorgeous (yet priceless) day.

Thinking I might have cerebral malaria (not good) or meningitis, my friend Michele tried her best to get us a lift to the clinic. Randi and Nate had the job of slapping me back to consciousness every few minutes—literally!

Oddly enough, a large brown spider had bitten my foot the night before, and it had swollen to the size of…well let's just say Shaquille O'Neal had nothing on me! The clinic was ironically out of generator fuel and could not simply test me for malaria (which we all knew I had). As I sat there with my gigantic foot and feverish demeanor, people walked by in awe of the white girl in the bush with the outrageously large foot. I couldn't help but laugh. No one else could, either. I would eventually get the proper treatment, but that would pale in importance to the encounter with Jesus that would usher in the heartbeat of my existence in one large whirlwind under Africa's infamous stars.

Awakened to a Movement

I staggered outside late in the night to view the legendary stars of Africa once more. All 50 children were sleeping, but one infant remained awake. Michele had him close to her heart. As we sat together, he made his way into my arms. As I snuggled baby Justice close, you guessed it—time for me stood still.

Here in this place, surrounded by intense war, there was peace. How tangible was it? Peace was embodied in this little baby. Justice's story mirrors God's heart for a lasting movement of love among nations immersed in warfare. What I did not tell you was that Justice came to the children's home on the brink of death. He was orphaned and malnourished, looking like little more than a skeleton. Within months, he was cooing, well-fed, and growing. What is more, he was living in the breathing reality of family.

While holding Justice that night, I began to dream. I began to ask the question, "What would happen if I gave my life for ones like these?" I began to understand that significant change within countries could be accomplished through the children. I asked, "What would happen if an entire generation in a war-torn nation were brought up differently?" They were the change their villages, communities, and nations were so desperately needing and looking for. Love looked like something. Here, Michele had captured it in one baby being rescued at a time.

Love Looks Like Something

What would that moment have looked like for Mary? The very second where a perceived promise became embodied and tangible right in front of her. What would her first night as a mother have looked like?

The sweat running down her face as evidence of sheer exhaustion seemed to fade away. A new quickening overshadowed the stomach-turning smells around her. She looked around at the oddity of surroundings. The dirt and debris were caking her ripped robe. There were shrieks from the livestock of bewilderment and intrigue at a new arrival on their turf. What was happening? Love was ripping into our realm.

In the midst of all this chaos, there was silence for Mary. In her gaze she marveled at the delicate baby in her arms. Her promise was now embodied. It was here. *He* was here. He really was here! She couldn't believe it.

There it was. This before-and-after moment was all in one glance. One minute, it was all for "someday." The next, it was here. And there was no turning back.

Mary began to contemplate again her first break-in from Heaven. She pondered the angel and majestic announcement. Then came the confusion, the staggering of words to attempt to explain the unnatural. The looks and glares from those who had heard the town gossip. She could see it and experience it all again.

All of those days of waiting and watching, wondering what this all would look like. Then, suddenly, here He was. Love looked like something.

Staring down at his little hands, she counted each just to make sure. She pondered, "How could God be so dependent? Why would He make Himself needy, helpless, and weak?"

Thus far, the journey looked nothing like she had imagined. Sitting there in the dirt, she wondered, "Where from here?" The Son of God was not born with a silver spoon in His mouth. He came naked, carrying only dependence and innocence at His side.

Mary began to dream. She wondered about His first steps. Where and how would they live? How would He become King and take His throne? How long would she have to wait to see the fulfillment of all she had been promised? What in the world was she supposed to do in the meantime?

The pain to get here was worth it. The suffering, exhaustion, and agony were now a mere afterthought. He was here. This was real. It was more than real. Mary's promise had pushed through to her world right in front of her eyes. She was holding in her lap the manifestation of Heaven's whispers.

Innately Given

But this wouldn't be the end. No, it was only the beginning. Where would she go from here? Where was the angel when she needed him? She could pray, but God hadn't learned to even crawl yet, much less talk. Where do we go when our promise is birthed and yet needs to be nurtured and cared for?

Mary was given the gifts to know how to mother her promise. She had no direction book, no idea, and no experience. Her mother wasn't even there to give answers! But within her was a gift innately given. It was who she had been created to be all along. This was who she was. It flowed through her veins from the moment she was made. She was meant to be a mother. Mary was meant to carry Heaven in all its messiness and beauty.

Who we've been created to be is uniquely natural to us. It looks completely insane to others—completely unnatural. And, at times, it seems completely stupid. But in Heaven's eyes, when He sees it, He calls it good. God gives us what we need along the way.

For Mary and for us thus far, the process of carrying and birthing a promise had been a bumpy journey. God was saying, "I want to engage with you, and I want you to engage with Me."

This, too, is for you. Who are you at the core of your being? What have you been destined for? Forget self-made dreams and plans. Forget fame and fortune and making yourself great. How can you be great in Heaven's eyes? Give yourself away freely. When we arrive at the place where we see our reflection in the eyes of Jesus, nothing else matters. No degree, no plan, no platform comes close.

In the end, it's for one thing and one thing only that we throw ourselves away for Him—Love's sake.

Children Will Carry the Kingdom

I woke up to the sound of waterfalls of rain pounding down on the metal roof above me. A new morning had emerged with even more to see. I could see an eyeball peeking underneath our blue metal door leading outside. Connecting with its gaze, a shriek of surprise-filled giggles burst from the little one realizing I was, in fact, awake. They were waiting for us.

We scuffled into a small room where the older children slept. There was no instruction needed for the children. They loved Jesus, and they knew exactly how to cause Him to run their way. While worshiping, God began to show me a picture of His Kingdom. Michele always calls them "castles in the mud." I knew that He wanted me to be a part of His Kingdom coming more to Africa. But as I tried to lift His throne and carry it to the earth, it was much too heavy for me.

Talia came up beside me in the vision and took the throne, placed it on her head (in Africa, women will carry almost everything on their heads), and carried it to the earth as if it were light as a feather.

Stunned, I stayed on the floor lingering to see more. I had the answer my heart had been looking for. God is calling for the childlike to flip the world on its head. He is searching for those who trust, those who will abandon everything just to follow Him—the poor in spirit who possess nothing and yet contain all who He is.

Jesus showed us the way to go.

> *At about the same time, the disciples came to Jesus asking, "Who gets the highest rank in God's kingdom?" For an answer Jesus called over a child, whom He stood in the middle of the room, and said, "I'm telling you, once and for all, that unless you return to square one and start over like children, you're not even going to get a look at the kingdom, let alone get in. Whoever becomes simple and elemental again, like this child, will rank high in God's kingdom. What's more, when you receive the childlike on My account, it's the same as receiving Me"* (Matthew 18:1-7).

What Will You Ask For?

While in Sudan, God began to ask us if we wanted a nation. I wasn't sure I knew what that meant. Inside of me, the promise was that exploited children throughout the earth would be rescued and restored to their innate innocence. He had put inside of me a heart to follow a movement led by children in the darkest places of the earth. In my own life, my desire is to propel a movement that challenges the current response of the world to need. Jesus restored justice to the hidden, the orphan, the forgotten, and the captive—that's us!

While in Sudan and Mozambique, I looked into the eyes of exploited children around the globe. I saw children enslaved, child soldiers in Africa, children trafficked in the sex trade in Asia, and children in the Middle East forced into the wars of their fathers.

What has He shown you? What is inside of you? What will you ask Him for? You can take your promise—that God has called you to missions, to transform a city, a nation, or a people group. It doesn't have to end there.

Has He called you to art? Has He led you to business? Is it science? God has called you and He will breathe upon you His Spirit to get the job done.

You've got the word, the promise, and the angel. Now what? Stick close to His heart. That rhythm will be the only thing that steers you correctly. There are times, though, in the waiting when it seems it is slowly fading away. But listen closely. It is there—beating, living, and thriving. When your reception is low, hold on to the small bar of connection that you have left.

Intimacy with Jesus—closeness to His heart—is the door to fruitfulness. Mary was not to create her promise. Her only responsibility was to feed it. Each day, she would need to give it living bread. You've got to feed your promise! Every day, especially in those times that you feel weak, feed it. Nourish it. Hydrate it. God has called you.

A New Tribe

Do we know what it is like to be children? Or, more than children, do we know the reality of being sons and daughters? There is always this tension between believing we are poor, needy, and servants and the idea that we are royalty and a part of the family. Can both exist together? Can a palace thrive in the mud? Can we be needy and princely at the same time? Or do we have to go through life in a schizophrenic mind-set? Am I a servant? Or am I a daughter?

How can all of these seeming opposites coexist in one accord? How is it possible for suffering to be married to joy? Why in the world would weakness and power need one another? Was Jesus a prince? Or was He a servant? He was both. His identity in Heaven determined what He would become on earth. He decided to leave the palace for the dirt in all its glory. He was a King who chose poverty. Who was He? He was rich but gave up all He had. Jesus is a ruler who gave up His crown for love's sake and didn't look back.

When God started speaking to me about the shaping of the promise He had given me, He showed me countless people who would give their lives away for tangible love. It was a tribe of people who lived, not for justice itself, but for the reality of a movement of tangible mercy being established to the ends of the earth. This new tribe is full of people like you and me. They are those who are unconcerned with fame or prestige. They are the little ones who, in their poverty, will reign with Jesus.

This new tribe will not settle. It will be a band of nomads running throughout the earth. These will be those who follow the Lamb wherever He goes. Always moving. They will find their home in Him alone. They are a modern-day people of the tent.

Living in Heaven's Laughter

What would our life look like if we lived in His gaze, in His delight? We were fashioned for love and created for enjoyment. I used to think that I had to push myself to become something. I thought that in order to be useful, I needed to work hard and give, give, give. I remember sitting in a bus going throughout eastern Africa and seeing human need like I had never before witnessed. Each kilometer we went, there was more to see. It was too much. It overwhelmed me. I felt small and weak, and did I mention frustrated?

God doesn't just smile when we sell everything we have and become poor in the most distraught areas of the world. He doesn't just jump for joy when we leave our corporate jobs for the slums. No, He smiles just seeing Himself in us. He laughs when we don't do things the exact right way. He loves it! He loves watching us jump out and try.

I remember watching a little girl I knew transition from crawling to walking. She was one of the most beautiful little girls I have ever met. Her free spirit excites me to see what she will mature into later. There she was, nearly approaching her first birthday. Her steps were wobbly—dangerous, even. But there was something about those shaky knees that made me burst with laughter. She was seeing something for the very first time in her life. It didn't matter if she had taken one step or five hundred. I was delighted just watching her boldness and tenacity. God looks for the same things in us. Not perfection, but weakness that overcomes. He simply watches for our willingness.

What is Heaven's laughter? What makes Him smile? I think God grins when He sees the look of wonder in our eyes. It is the gaze that forgets about everything but Him. That little girl—we'll just call her Faith—had her eyes set on her dad as she took her first wobbly steps. Nothing else mattered to her. She put all that she was into learning to walk and throwing all she was in his direction.

Heaven can smile over the dust—over ordinary things and places of little earthly importance. It doesn't have to be a church or a building. In Mary's life, Heaven smiled in a dirt-filled cave. Heaven wants to ravish us with joy. Enough joy to defeat any sickness, any fear, and any danger that lies ahead. What keeps us from our promises? What causes some to die, while others seem to flourish? What is keeping you?

- I told you in the beginning that I was going to take you on a roller coaster ride. It is an expedition with many ups and downs. Thus far I have taken you or some of the highs and maybe over a few bumps in the road. But there is much more to see. There is much more to wade through and experience. God will give us joy, and plenty of it. Rolland Baker always says, "God is in a good mood!" It's true He is. Yet joy is a by-product of suffering. Opposites always take on cause and effect roles in Heaven's Kingdom. Ashes give way to beauty. Mourning transitions into laughter. Sickness moves into healing, and so on. Oddly enough, they all work together at opposite poles.

Chapter 6

A Poor Man's Cup

"The poor anywhere in the world are Christ who suffers. In them, the Son of God lives and dies. Through them, God shows His face." —Mother Teresa

What is it that keeps us from living in the light of our promises? What stands between you and what God has placed inside of you? Do we decide to feed, encourage, and nourish what God has placed within us? Or do we instead at times stifle and try to hide it from view? I wonder if Mary's promise ever embarrassed her.

When we carry Heaven, when we are called to an outrageous life of fellowship with God from the outside in, people around us notice we are starting to "show." What is our reaction to their stares? We can hide, or we can share our promise. One thing is for sure. At times the process of watching our dream emerge from within us to the outside world can feel pretty awkward.

There were many consequences that could have stopped Mary from pursuing what God had handpicked her to bring into the earth. Think about it. She, out of all of us, had plenty of valid excuses! She was so very young in age. Her culture would absolutely reject the idea altogether. It would ruin all the plans she had made for herself. There was no earthly logic to what she had been given to do. Remember her first "yes"? Remember her agreement to follow after the heartbeat of her promise? That "yes" would indeed *continue* to cost her everything.

But what would that "everything" be? What would she have to face head-on just to follow after her promise each day at a time? Her family, her friends, her plans, and her dreams would all be compromised for the sake of this incredible undertaking. Her fiancé-turned-husband would have a choice to stick with her or leave. Mary's entire life would be turned upside down. What would she be asked or forced to give up? Who could she trust with her promise?

What stands between you and your destiny? False ideas about ourselves and lies we have believed can block us from experiencing what we have been called to walk in—fullness. At times, there is this temptation to settle for normalcy that is safe and stable—lifestyles that require no risks of failure or pain. Our family expectations can limit us to living in the same shadow and patterns of those who have gone before us out of fear, guilt, or false honor and obligation.

What pushed Mary on? What keeps us on the road toward finding what God has placed within us? The answer is simple—encounter.

We have all been hand-picked to bridge Heaven and earth. There is a new movement of God breathing across the earth today. We will not get there by riding on the coattails of those we elevate as "super saints." There is no magic formula we can buy, no secret side door to sneak through. We cannot get there through piggybacking off the experiences, the concepts, and the ideologies of others. The only way in is through His heart. No shortcuts can pass us through unseen. This journey will be messy. A lifestyle of following after God's heartbeat in the earth was never described as neat and orderly...or balanced for that matter! There are always unexpected twists and turns. But one thing's for sure. We are never alone.

Pushing on toward the unveiling of our promise is fueled with meeting with Jesus. It will not always be a mystical experience. Most of us will not recognize these times for what they are because we are expecting something completely different. We must learn to recognize Jesus in whatever form He comes to us.

I was surprised in some of the most unthought-of places where Jesus would show Himself to me. How do we find the face of Jesus? Sometimes that is the wrong question. In many instances, it is Jesus who is looking to find us. Where are we looking for Him in our own lives?

I entered the Middle East thinking that I would experience God's presence more than anywhere else on earth. It was, after all, where the world all began. Right? It wasn't until leaving that I realized that I had already found His home. I found Him in the poor, the needy, anyone really who said "yes" to all of who He is. His visitations were drawing to a close. It was now the beginning of the time of habitation where Heaven would find its dwelling place in empty ones who would yield themselves to Heaven's agenda and not their own.

50,000 Miles Later

Lifting off the narrow dirt airstrip in Sudan, we waved good-bye to Michele and the kids. Looking down below, we could see the Nile River, this time rushing forcefully upside down, unlike anywhere else on earth. We were heading south to Uganda. As our feet touched the ground, our direction would be turned completely around.

Overlooking Lake Victoria's shore once more, we spent the day praying about where to go. Randi had been given a vision about Israel. We had tried to bus north through northern Sudan and Egypt, but because of the war we were blocked from continuing. Now here we were, stuck in Uganda, wondering how we could get to the Middle East.

There on our faces, lying on our *kapulanas*, my phone began to ring. On the other end of the line was a stranger. He said he was calling from Croatia. Where in the world was Croatia? He burst forth quickly, attempting to finish his idea in one long, drawn-out breath. God had spoken to him about us, and he wanted to give us money to get to where we were headed next. I about fell on the ground. Good thing I was already down there to begin with!

Within days, we were in the air headed north to Israel. Where would we stay? What would it be like? What were we getting ourselves into?

Hours later, we touched down in Tel Aviv's large airstrip. So far, so good. Then it happened. I should have known better than to think that everything would go smoothly. It never had before. Why would it start now?

Exiting the plane, there we were. Three young adults who looked more like peasants than touristy Westerners. With our flip-flops—which were still covered with clumps of mud and remnants of Africa—we made our way off the plane. Thinking back, I am sure we would have looked out of place. Capri pants, sandals, a guitar, and no coats.

That wasn't the end of it. Three young adults with scruffy backpacks— one of them a young guy with dreadlocks, piercings, and tattoos—didn't fit the "rich American" motif. What was our welcoming entourage? They were none other than three armed Israeli guards. What were our motivations in coming to Israel, we were asked. Somehow our tourism answer didn't seem to fit with our outward appearance. The truth was we had very little money. And we were still about two hours from Jerusalem.

We managed to get away, only to find that Nate's camera and a few other items had been stolen out of his backpack. Thus far, this morning was not going in our favor.

It gets better. Another key piece of information that I forgot to check was what the weather would be like in Israel in March. That's right. Stepping off the plane, we saw snowflakes descending onto the black ground outside. No coats and bare feet—what a perfect combination!

Jumping on the bus line that ran throughout the new city of Jerusalem, we had no idea which direction we were traveling. Our taxi driver had knowingly dropped us off at the wrong location. On the bus next to us was a lone package. Instantly, the bus came to a halting stop and everyone was made to evacuate. We watched as armed and frantic officials swarmed the package attempting to identify its origin and contents. A bomb scare would leave us yet again walking up and down the infamous side roads.

Wandering the bustling streets of Jerusalem, we were quickly made aware that our contact had fallen through. Suddenly our plans became interrupted and crushed. We had no agenda, no plan, no security, and now, no place to sleep.

Homeless

Where would we stay? We were going to be stuck in Israel for the next month with nowhere to live. You would have thought that with the outrageous provision God had already given to us, our "faith-o-meters" would have been overwhelmed with belief that would turn the city upside down. Somehow, my brain was emptied of all memories of miracles and unforgettable equipping and supplies. All I was focused on was the fear of sleeping in the snow that night!

We panicked. After walking up and down Jaffa Street for hours, we sat down outside of a bank and huddled close together as icy air whipped through our T-shirts. Randi wanted to pray. "Forget praying!" I thought. I wanted to scream! I suppose God would have accepted either one at that moment. Suddenly, the dirt-covered paths of Africa seemed a distant luxury. I wanted to go back to our "home."

Knowing only a few words in Hebrew, I quickly realized that each answer to our questions was being politely answered in falsehood. We were getting nowhere! Looking around at our frigid surroundings, we made up our minds once more to keep going. Where? We had no idea. We slung our backpacks around our shoulders and continued to the Mount of Olives nearby…and by nearby I mean *forever* away!

Succat Hallel is the house of prayer that had been started by Rick Redding. We knew of this place from its international renown. Since it was a 24-hour room of prayer, we made our way there in hopes of putting ourselves in a place where God could help us.

Music filled the air, and thankfully, some heat, too! People crowded the room. Walking in, I whispered, "God, please give us a home."

Worship has a way of making me forget the barriers that limit me, you know? I tossed my backpack on the ground, kicked off my flip-flops, and was instantly submerged in God's presence. I didn't care anymore about the fears that seemed to quench my being so far that day. It was all worth it—the constant traveling, the sickness, the pain, the tears, the fears, and the constant unknowns. They all became blurry when He came near me.

Sometimes explaining worship can be so mystical and abstract that it is hard to embrace it as tangible and solid, something that we can reach out and catch for ourselves. That afternoon we had plenty of reasons to flip out and quit. If I were to be honest with you, though, quitting was no longer an option. We were beyond the ability to just "throw in the towel" and go "home" to our warm bubble baths and five-course meals. We had nothing. We were stuck in our "yes." Our choice had already been given a long time ago.

So there I was on the floor, immersed in this thick realization that Jesus was right beside me. As I saw His face, do you know what He was doing? He was laughing! Not simply the kind of chuckles that one hushes behind his composed demeanor. He was rolling with hysterics. So much so that I saw tears well up and stream down His face. Teardrops of intense joy and pleasure. He was relishing in utter euphoria. But why was that? And would I be offended?

How could God possibly laugh when so much hell had been released in the world around us? How could Jesus giggle in hilarity when pain was sweeping the earth each second that ticked by? The truth is, God is in a good mood. Being homeless seemed like utter defeat in my eyes. He knew what that was like! Why on earth would Jesus burst with laughter in the midst of unanswered questions we had been shouting all day long?

I knew it was Him because of His eyes. They were those same eyes that encompass the most conflicting of ideas. They were eyes that conveyed a message without words. Jesus wiped the tears of glee from His cheeks and reached His hands out toward me. With a wisp, He touched His tear-drenched finger to my forehead. Without warning, I was on the floor—this young girl in sandals and a tank top in the middle of Israel's winter. What an odd sight to see. I rolled and spun in unrestrained laughter. I couldn't stop! In that moment, I'm not sure I would have wanted to knock it off anyway.

My mind couldn't understand. I couldn't process Jesus' heart. But I could catch it. When I did, nothing else came close to captivating my attention. Wait a minute! I was stranded in the Middle East with nowhere to go. "Who cares?" I thought. I was caught in the midst of Heaven jumping into my world. Nothing else mattered. I wanted to stay in this place forever. Forget changing the world—I needed to be changed, too!

We stuck out like sore thumbs. I looked over and Randi was in her usual state—glued to the floor in a heap. A few people in front motioned for us to come forward for prayer. "Great," I thought. I wondered if they assumed we needed deliverance at that rate!

We couldn't get up but managed to crawl to the front, dragging one another along the way. A group of people began praying for us. Those near us held us up in an effort to lift us from the ground. As those around us began to pray, I felt like buckets of water were pouring over my head with little relenting. Within nanoseconds, we were both back on the floor, plastered as if merged to the tile beneath us.

No one knew us. At best, to those around us, we were these outrageous-looking young people who didn't even know how to dress in the extreme cold. What came next would again shatter our boxes of God's plans for our lives.

The man's words rang through the air around us. *"You will be forerunners for your generation. You both will begin houses for children throughout the world. I see Africa. Many, many children are coming!"* What was happening? All I know is that I was fixed to the floor baffled at the words that were being spoken over us. No one knew us. They had no idea where we had been, why we were there, or where we were going. Yet in the midst of the holy chaos that we found ourselves in, what would our response be? Laughter.

On the ground, Randi and I in a pile of pitiful hilarity looked more like complete simpletons than anything else. Looking back on that day, I'm sure it must have looked like a theme park attraction. We were a mess. But oh, was it fun!

When Heaven Answers

Time seemed as if it were spinning into oblivion. Hours later, after being revived off the floor, we reclined in a couple plastic chairs, trying to make even a little sense of what had just happened to us. People continued to circle us, yet this time they asked us where we had come from.

Finally feeling like I was alert enough to process what was going on, I looked at Randi. The look in her eyes was full of wonder and a slight twinge of embarrassment. I knew the feeling well. What had just happened?

As I looked up, a blonde-haired lady had been sitting by us the entire time. I noticed her accent as being from South Africa. She introduced herself to us, and without as much as breath between, said, "I don't know why, but I feel like God told me to have you come and stay with me at my house. Do you have a place to stay while here?"

I looked over at Nate, who was still making fun of us for the fiasco that we had been in hours earlier. His eyes widened. God has just answered our fears. We thought that we had to do something to help or make something happen to bring the answer to ourselves. We did nothing. While we were glued to the tile, looking like fools and getting touched by even more of His heart, Jesus was doing what only He could do. He took care of us again. Perhaps that was why He was giggling in the beginning. What seemed like a mountain before us looked like an insignificant molehill in His eyes. We were floored. Quite literally!

Bombs in the Background

The home so graciously offered to us was at the top of the city, and the view was breathtaking. Thousands of stone stairs built the city upward. Down below, life seemed bustling but cautious. Bomb sirens flooded the air. It would come to be a fading backdrop in the month we would spend there.

We would race up and down the stone stairs. Nate counted one day to discover nearly a thousand just on the way up! That day we were to meet with a couple from Africa who had begun an amazing work in the heart of Bethlehem.

Entering the Old City, I felt like I was being hurled back into Bible times. Our new friends had given us shawls to drape around our bare shoulders. The constant stair climbing kept our blood temperature high enough to manage to make it through the cold, whipping wind.

Aaron and Brenda were intense, to say the least. Sitting in a seat within one of the old city's stone buildings, we waited to meet them. Without as much as a hello, they grabbed us into massive hugs and began speaking words into our lives that left us speechless and in a state of shock.

Going around the circle from Nate to Randi to myself, they basically read our mail! *"Mommas to the nations,"* they shouted. *"You will preach with fire, unlock the captives, forerunners.* " They continued for what seemed like hours as we sat there amazed at the bombshell of surprise that was hitting us. Aaron and Brenda didn't have a clue about who we were. Their prophetic firing squad hit us with a force that seemed to pin us back in our seats. We were being reminded that God had been in control all along.

The Wailing Wall

With my hands gripping onto the ancient stones that made the wall what it was, I noticed pieces of paper crammed and stuffed into tiny crevices in between the stones. They were prayers given in utter need and hunger. As I closed my eyes, I instantly saw Jesus. He looked hungry, sleep-deprived, and tired—exhausted, really. The look in His eyes startled me. They looked desperate. He took a hold of my shoulders and looked into my eyes. He said, "I am hungry for My Bride, and I will not rest until I have her."

I had never before encountered Jesus in the state He was in. He looked beaten down, almost beyond recognition. He didn't look regal but ragged. He didn't look like a celebrity. He looked like a "nobody." My head spun as I thought about what He had forcefully said to me. Heaven's hunger is contagious. He was dying for love. His sole purpose was a desire to be joined to us.

Not knowing how long I had been there, I opened my eyes to glance around me. As I looked up, right above me were two cooing doves.

Kingdom Refugees

Her breath was growing heavier, but the sound of her heart pounding in fear overwhelmed and drowned out her feelings of extreme exhaustion. Nearly tripping, she looked down as her sandals flung in the wind, broken from the rocks she had to climb. There was no time. No seconds available where she could even think about saying "no." It was no longer about her anymore. She had been given something that would change the world. This was no longer about her dreams, her safety, or her desires. It was not about *her* anymore.

This was now much larger than Mary. She was now a part of something that transcended herself and even her interpretation and expectations surrounding her promise. No, in this instant, her promise was vulnerable, and her obedience would be His only protection from the whirlwind of threat and danger that was heading their way. One minute, all of Heaven was smiling down on them in majesty and splendor. The next, all the lights, celestial electricity, and glitz hit a sudden blackout. They were gone. And once again, Mary was left at another crossroads in her life.

Jesus had crashed into humanity's world naked and weak. Really going for that shock factor, eh? There He was, in her arms. In those moments, Mary realized that the pain was worth it. Little did she know, this was only the beginning. These fleeting moments of basking in her promise would be short-lived, at least for now. After the angelic choir had been silenced, after the shepherds made their way back to their lives in the fields, once the wise men were on their camels, headed home empty-handed, she was there, alone with Joseph and this tiny dependent life that was now completely at her mercy. What now?

Her great birth announcement rang through the Heavens. Yet minutes later, there was silence. This 15 minutes of fame lasted for just that. All she could hear in the world around her were the normal sounds of busy lives. The great star in the East was dimmed. When the lights went out, there she was, sitting once again in a place of decision, a place of questioning, and a place of great wonder.

What do we do when the lights go down, when truth is all that is left before us? Nothing can dress us up to be more than we are in those moments. The curtain is drawn and the ones who join us start back, following their own lives again. When the lights fade around our promise, we are given another choice to say "yes" once more. Most of the time, when we experience and go through the messy birthing of what God has put inside of us, we assume ignorantly that this is *it*. Maybe we think we've "made" it. This is our chance, our shot, we think. The truth is, this "it" moment lasts only for a few breaths, and then it is gone. This is just the beginning. What happens *after* begins a lifelong journey on a low road that few of us know exist.

Heaven welcomed Jesus and relished in His coming. The earth would not take them in, but forced them out—deported. From His first small breaths into humanity's home, He would be dragged to the margins, across borders, and thrown into a land of exile.

This time, ole Joe himself had a visitation from an angel. It was not a favor-filled run-in with Heaven, but an urgent warning. "Leave your country now," the angel burst forth. "Your life and the life of the baby are on the line. Go to Africa. Don't hesitate; leave now."

There was no time to say good-bye to their families. Under the cover of darkness, they would run and cross the border into a land they had never before tread. This would be a defining moment in their lives—a time of no turning back.

Check this out! God makes Himself dependent on a couple of teenagers! What was Mary thinking? With fear, confusion, and questioning God's promise and protection, did she wonder, "Where is God in this?"

Within days of making His understated entrance, Jesus was crossing national borders, becoming a sojourner Himself! His first immersion—a new baptism if you will—was into the mud, into the nations, and into the margins. God's baptism into the nations is an invitation for you and me as well. He is looking for those who will choose the margins—the edges of society—just as He did. This fulcrum of a movement that is circling the earth is in the lives of the broken. Are we willing to go anywhere to find Him?

Caught on Film

Along the cobblestone streets, we made our way through the narrow alleyways that make the old city of Jerusalem breathtaking. The culture and the colors that waft throughout those open-air corridors bring such mystery and wonder. I had this feeling of being transported back in time. The smells of Middle Eastern spices and foods simmering engulfed the tiny tunnels. Large strips of dyed fabrics waved as air gusted through from the entrances inside. Entering in was like stepping into an entirely different world. The underground movement of life was in full swing.

Haggling is one of my favorite pastimes. I love learning enough of a language to barter in it. It's one of the simple pleasures of my life! As I was negotiating with an Arab man over a warmer shawl, Randi rolled her eyes, confused at how fair arguing could be enjoyable. I was enthralled in the moment like a kid in a candy store.

As we made our way out of the tunnels to the open air, the Dome of the Rock was filling the background behind us. I draped my new thick shawl around Randi and myself to huddle in for more warmth. Wading through the people, a microphone was thrown unexpectedly in our faces.

An Israeli news reporter and camera crew was conducting surveillance in the crowded streets. Again, something made us stand out. "What is the hope of Israel?" he asked. "You've got to be kidding me!" I thought. We were on national television being interviewed without even being asked. What was Israel's hope? What should be their expectancy?

Without even a hesitation we chimed in. There we were, flip-flopped young radicals preaching on television to a nation. Israel did have a hope. It wasn't the Jesus who had been cartooned for a "made for television" special. He was real, and He desired them as His own—within their own culture.

Floating in the Dead Sea

The horizon looked like a picture on a postcard, the colors so deep that one's eyes could not possibly translate it to fullness. The Jordan valley was blooming this time of year. Flowers and tall, lush green and golden grasses filled the hillsides in front of us. Mountains covered the backdrop of the Dead Sea.

I dipped my toes into the water, expecting frigid temperatures. We were far enough away from Jerusalem to catch a warm front. The water was thermal and inviting. Noticing that I didn't flinch when inching in, Nate ran and cannonballed right into the deep blue and brown expanse.

The Dead Sea is set apart from all the other bodies of water in the world. Nothing living can exist within it. With such high quantities of salt, you can float. It was one of the weirdest feelings I have ever experienced. Jumping in, I watched Nate floating by cross-legged. I laughed as he held his hands up in circles as if meditating on top of the waters.

As Randi glided into the water, she shrieked in pain. We had all gotten cuts, abrasions, and other wounds along the way. As she lunged in, the salt immersed her open wounds. It hurt! But it healed quickly.

Our Dead Sea escapade turned out to be deeper than I had imagined. It was a call to baptism for us. It was an immersion and initiation into a life of utter abandon. We were no longer our own. We were being invited into the death and resurrection of our promise. Welcomed, if you will, into a life of living from Jesus' heart—the beautiful, the unlovely, and the unimaginable real-life unfolding of Heaven on earth in our lives in each place He would send us.

The Poor in Spirit

No one would take us to the West Bank. It was too dangerous, we were told. I knew we were supposed to get there before our time in Israel was up. Our friend Meravi decided that she would take us one day as we were wading in the Jordan River.

Shiloh contained the temple ruins where Hannah would bring her offerings in the Old Testament book of First Samuel. Hannah's story merges with ours. She was barren and could have no children of her own. She was empty—literally! The very thing that she was created to do was impossible for her! Her promise was out of reach, and there was no natural road to get there.

Hannah did not linger in her emptiness. She went after an invisible, an impossible promise. She ran to the temple to jump into God's lap. What was her strategy? She lay at His feet and asked Him for her destiny. She reached beyond the stars to the One who had created them so long ago.

Hannah was poor in spirit. Her prayer was simple. "God, bring forth in me Your promise. Let me bridge Heaven and earth. Use me as a conduit. Embody my vow and I will give it back to You. Let me hold a son in my arms and he will be Yours forever." Her cries reached Heaven.

While sitting in the temple ruins where Hannah prayed, it was as if her cries came back to life. She looked intoxicated she was so distraught. Wailing and weeping ushered in her promise. She asked, and God gave. That was as simple as it could get.

The impossible suddenly became possible. The unnatural instantly turned commonplace and normal. Upside down transforms to right side up. What does it mean to be poor in spirit? Why was Hannah answered? Why did God give Hannah her heart's desire? Poverty of spirit is a place of knowing our spiritual need. It is a location where we realize just how much we need Heaven to enter our lives. It is where we learn dependence and weakness—an awakening to who we are not and who He is. It is a union where opposites attract. We give God our weakness, He gives power. We surrender our brokenness to Heaven, and it fills and mends the holes deep within our hearts. We toss our hunger His way, and He meets us with bread from Heaven that brings fullness like we have never known before. The poor in spirit give God room to complete them. It's not a hidden and expensive secret of the ages. It is a blatant invitation to more. To get there, though, we must be willing to unveil our vulnerability and become transparent.

What will cries like Hannah's look like in our day? God is raising up a new generation from the dust. These waves will not fade, but deepen. This journey is not about *us* anymore. An ageless vow echoes through time. With this invitation comes an opportunity. Our open door to living in Heaven's shadow begins to open up before us.

Jesus via Satellite

We were sitting on pillows in the glass room overlooking Jerusalem. All four walls were glass, allowing us to see every direction across the city. Night was falling across the horizon in our time zone. Oceans away, afternoon was in full swing in the United States.

Randi and I were invited to minister at a church meeting in Kentucky via satellite from Israel. It was one in the morning our time and seven at night in the states. We had never ministered via computer before, but we were expectant and eager to see what would happen.

The videos were on, and there we were on the big screen. We ushered in the presence of Jesus. Worship was amazing, and we found ourselves on the floor unable to get in view of the camera. As Jesus swept the rooms both in Israel, where we were, and in North America, I marveled at His presence and love from a distance thousands of miles away—an entire ocean away! We prophesied and shared the promises that we saw within the lives of individuals there in the room for about six hours. The Holy Spirit fell on the people who were gathered, and many were on their faces.

I felt like we were in some kind of dream. Somehow, God loved our hunger so much that He would span oceans and time zones just to be with us.

His Cup

As the Sabbath fell on the eve of Passover, the entire city of Jerusalem grew silent. One minute I heard children giggling and playing on the tops of their homes. The next, all of life was still. The glass room became our dining area. As we lounged, the short table was filled with wine, cheese, bread, and other foods spanning its length.

Our friends told us a story to help us enter into the Passover meal. In their hands, one friend held up a glass of wine. "In Jewish custom, when a man falls in love with a woman, his marriage proposal was not done on one knee, or even with a ring," she said. "He would set a cup of wine before the one he loved. If the young beauty was, in fact, interested in her beloved—if she was pleased with him—she would drink from the cup."

Drinking from her lover's cup meant that she would follow him, join herself to him, and become one with who he was. It was part of her wedding vows—in good times and in bad, she would press onward in her journey with the one she loved. She would choose the good and the bad, the blissful times and the hard, aching moments, all because of love.

Jesus' cup remains set in front of us, awaiting our answer. It is not a cup of prestige or fame, but one of lowliness and hiddenness. Not a shiny golden cup, but a chalice recycled from ageless surrender. As I was hearing the story, I watched a picture of myself cupping my hands, receiving from Jesus. I became the glass that held all that He was. He would take my thirst and my emptiness and fill me up. He would pour out in our lives richness and need, joy and suffering—all of these in one.

Heaven is not merely looking for those who will say "yes" to drinking from His cup, but those who will together make their home in Him. He is looking for a people of the tent who will follow the Lamb wherever He goes—those who will resign themselves to a life of wandering. This is a nomadic lifestyle where we venture together as one tribe. Find Your home in us, Jesus.

Living in Love

There are days when we are full of joy and life is beautiful. There are other days where you can feel horrible and out of control. That's the crazy nature of this upside-down, inside-out Kingdom that we have stepped into. There is something about this process of carrying the promise where God desires to grow more love in you. And He wants to know what you are saying to Him. Do you have a response to your call? In a day and age bewitched in the preservation of self, these echoes are beginning to stir once more. "No man lives unto himself. We were born to live for someone else."[1]

What shall we sing? What will our song be? Will it be a new anthem to our King that gives our allegiance to Him alone? This anthem that God is conducting throughout the earth is a new battle cry, yet one that has echoed from the earliest of time. "That the Lamb may receive the reward for His suffering."[2]

When we begin to live out of being in love with Jesus, things around us will change. They will not change because of who we are, but *Who* we have joined ourselves to. When we become enthralled by Heaven's scent, we carry with us an aroma that will literally shake nations. This fragrance is much stronger than the early morning smell of rich coffee—it will awaken even the deepest of sleepers. Have you been awakened?

A Wasted Life

Jesus made His heart clear for us in Luke:

> *Anyone who intends to come with Me has to let Me lead. You're not in the driver's seat—I am. Don't run from suffering; embrace it. Follow Me and I'll show you how. Self-help is no help at all. Self-sacrifice is the way, My way, to finding yourself, your true self. What good would it do to get everything you want and lose you, the real you? ... This isn't, you realize, pie in the sky by and by. Some who have taken their stand right here are going to see it happen, see with their own eyes the kingdom of God* (Luke 9:23-27).

In the beginning, the charge that still echoes in my memory from Jesus has always remained: "As I rescued you, rescue them." I thought in that moment that I understood the density of such a command. Later, I was given a taste of the intensity that those words carried within their meaning.

I was always mesmerized with stories of miracles around the world. Remember my first week in Mozambique? There we were, barefoot in the dirt and in the middle of the African bush. That night under the dim light that we rigged to the truck, I watched as God healed a blind man in front of my very eyes. The look in this older man's eyes as I watched the cataracts fall and the color of his irises change from blue to gray to brown tattooed my memory with a burning desire to know this reality more. In its wake, it left an imprint of expectancy and hope. It was the simplicity of Jesus in our midst. No need for human intervention or prestige. Only a willing, humble, and broken heart was required.

A broken life carries with it an aroma that attracts the very presence of Jesus among us. It is the reality of His heart for the marginalized, the nobodies, the weak, the overlooked, the underqualified, the downcast, the condemned, and the poor. That is each of us! These are those who become the location where Jesus dwells. It is on the margins where we see Him for who He really is in one face at a time.

I have plenty of those stories, and many of them we will continue to relive together. Those memories, however, are only part of the picture of the journey that I have walked and come to know thus far. The truth is, miracles are only a small portion of a life that is laid down for Love—a life stemmed from an outrageous relationship with God. Most of the time, we are sold this small percentage as if it were the entire story. There is much more on the other side of what we have been told. It is a reality that we can only know by encountering it ourselves.

Early on, I was informed that the Gospel was both suffering and joy. I embraced this idea with complete ignorance and assumed that it merely meant that the suffering would be leaving behind the fast-food chains of America. (Oh, and hot showers!) I concluded that the "suffering" was equivalent to the inconvenience of missionary life. You know, the typical things such as makeup running down your face in the hot tropical heat, bad hair days, mosquitoes, and no television. I was wrong.

Endnotes

1. "Receive," written and sung by Cindy Ruakere, www.cindyruakere.com.

2. The Moravian Missions Banner Cry.

Chapter 7

Love Has a Cost

For none of us lives to himself… (Romans 14:7 NKJV).

"If you learn to get low, God will give you the earth."[1] A prolific life of carrying Heaven to earth cascades down through us from the low place. What is the low place? How do we get there? The low place is a seat with the humble—the meek. It is found with the nobodies of our villages, our towns, our cities, and our nations. Its whereabouts are located on the margins, beyond the gates, in a place of need and hunger.

We have been summoned to embrace a new movement of God in the world. What is this movement? What will it look like? And why would God choose nobodies like you and me? This new drifting will be found on the sidelines of commercial and modern politics and faith agendas. It will be a 180-degree turn from what we have expected and known before. Our grids will be smashed. Our drafted directions will get us nowhere. The front door that we have attempted to unlock and squeeze through before will stay locked. The back door, hidden and camouflaged, will blow open with wild winds of change. God will turn us on our heads and ask us to go low instead of climb up. The ladder of success will suddenly become barren. Our longing will be to follow in the barefoot trail of Jesus from the bottom up.

You were made to bear fruit that will bring sustenance and life to others. "Fruitfulness flows from intimacy with God and it flows from a place of yielded love."[2] It costs us something.

What is intimacy with God? What does an intimate life look like? For many of us, the thought of uncovered closeness seems scary. To be vulnerable and honest with someone who knows everything about us seems too exposing to handle. For some of us, past experiences have taught us that intimacy is controlling, dominant—something that steals from us who we are in our weakness. Experience tells some of us that being vulnerable means that we lose something dear to us. Being transparent, according to our history, means being exploited instead of protected—stripped instead of covered.

Legitimate intimacy with Jesus means that we draw close to Him. We are invited to join Him as His friends—Heaven's sons and daughters. We become one with who He is. We are welcomed into His arms and asked to receive part of His nature. We reflect His image, and His likeness forever masks our stare.

God created you and I with two things in mind. He wanted to be with us and flow through us. What is fruitfulness? Fruitfulness is a place of union where we transition from being carriers of Heaven to residents and conduits. We begin to be overflowed with God in us and pour out to those around us. An intimate life means sticking close to Heaven's whispers.

Evacuating Israel

We were scheduled to fly from Israel back to Uganda in two days' time. The days were getting colder, and, walking through the streets of Jerusalem that day, we stopped in a market nearby. The stalls were filled with a rainbow of colors. Fruits that we recognized and those that we had never before encountered overflowed the aisles.

Randi and I danced around the aisles as if caught in a dream. We couldn't believe this was our life! How had we gotten here? Why would God let us see miracles in the dirt of Africa and in the dust of the Middle East? With the sun hidden from sight, we felt the warmth of Heaven smiling down on us. I was realizing that we were loved. Loved beyond our wildest imaginations.

After climbing another thousand-stone stairs that led us to the top of the city, we crashed into our friend's home, freezing from the cold and blood boiling from the intense workout we had just experienced. Without a pause, our friend gave us alarming news. We thought we were scheduled to fly out the next morning. After reading our itinerary, we realized that we were really intended to leave on a red-eye flight that very evening. That was only in a few hours. We were already two hours from the airport. Our few clothes were filthy, and nothing was packed. (Although, as you know by now, that wouldn't have taken long anyway!) To make things worse, Nate was gone in Jerusalem somewhere down below. We had no way of contacting him. We looked at each other in astonishment. Would we miss our plane?

Randi and I scurried to the bedroom to toss our belongings back into our small backpacks and Nate's. We frantically changed into a pair of dusty clothes and kicked on our flip-flops. When Nate arrived home with a look of peace across his face, we threw him in our friend's car and headed for the airport.

Rushing two hours to Tel Aviv was impossible. There was no earthly way we would have gotten to the plane on time. Waiting in the airport were our infamous "friends"—the same Israeli guards who spent so much time interrogating us before. With weird smirks on their faces, they instantly stopped us.

Our small bags were searched twice over as if we were hiding something. An angry guard asserted that I had forged an American passport. Apparently, my last name meant "gold and light" in Hebrew, which in this guy's mind proved that I was secretly a Jewish refugee posing as an American. Sure, I was a Middle Eastern girl with a twangy country accent—this was unbelievable!

After I convinced the officials that I was indeed a small-town, albeit forgetful, Westerner, they allowed us to finally get on the plane—dirty, aggravated, and exhausted. What more could happen in this crazy ride that we now called our lives?

Riots, Potholes, and Disaster

Touching down once more in Africa's familiar red dirt, we were in store for a road trek of disastrous proportions. Thirteen insanely erratic happenings would take place in the next 53 hours of our lives that none of us could have predicted.

Riots were pounding Kampala city as we touched down in Uganda. Afraid we were going to miss our bus, our friend Peace hid our foreign faces from the sight of the streets and took a back way to the bus station. The streets were crowded with panicked, fighting, and screaming bodies. A delayed bus forced us to hide for another three hours in the hot African sun.

Our first breakdown happened three hours into our journey. For three more hours, we were stranded on the side of the road in the middle of nowhere in Uganda. We were scheduled to travel through three countries, arriving in the eastern coastal city of Dar Es Salaam in Tanzania in just 24 hours. Our road trip would last nearly three days, as chaos ensued every hour on the hour.

Starting back on the "road," we hit a gigantic hole in the road that blew out our front two tires. We were stuck again for two more grueling hours, this time in the start of our first night on the road. We arrived at the Kenyan border in the middle of the night and were welcomed by no one. No guards were there! Everyone was gone. It looked like a ghost town. Without the possibility to get our visas into Kenya, we had to sleep at the border through the night.

At 5:30 A.M., we started off across Kenya's border. There was only one problem. Our bus kept breaking down. The driver kept pulling over in hopes to jumpstart the rickety bus. One passenger jumped off with her bag and started walking at a faster speed than the bus was going! I thought about following her. We might have made it across the next two countries faster if so!

Soon, we approached a tiny mud road with hundreds of trucks. There was a major traffic jam ahead of us. This was our only route to get through the country, so we had to trek on. Suddenly, our bus became stuck in the mud for hours. We were asked to get off and push!

Once out of the mud, we were blocked by a police checkpoint, and with our unbelievable luck, we were stopped. Instantly, armed guards rushed the bus and ripped our driver out of his seat. They took him away into a nearby mud building. We were stuck in the middle of Kenya with no driver and had no idea why he had been taken away.

Hours later, we finally coasted into the city of Nairobi. It was already night and over 24 hours later. Our bus was again delayed, and we had to sleep in the terminal all night.

At 1:00 A.M., the officials told 15 of us that we could go with another bus that night. When the rest of the dozens of others who were declined heard of the limit, they staged a mutiny and all jumped on the bus together. Soon the police were called. Officers came and started ripping people off the bus. In the midst of that chaos, we got a new bus and left at 3:00 A.M.

When morning came, we exited our seats to finally grab a banana on a break. When we stepped back onto the bus, we were shocked that two foreign girls on safari stole our seats and threw our bags in the back, which meant that we had to sit by the toilet for 12 hours!

This ride got better. Soon after beginning again, the left side of the bus's windshield cracked, broke off, and then fell out onto the road in front of us. There we were—holding on for dear life as wind blasted us. And wouldn't you know, we came upon yet another police check.

When we came to a stop, a man who was nervous (or had a breakdown from the three-day torture session) snapped, jumped out of the window, and started running down the road frantically. A few men chased him down and tied him to a chair in front of us with a leather belt. We were pretty confused by this point. But the fact that we were so incredibly exhausted kept us from even asking.

Going throughout Tanzania's countryside, rain began pelting down hard upon us, and water flooded the inside of the bus. We were beginning to get drenched! On the upside, I guess we should have been thankful for the faux shower.

Three days later, we rolled into Tanzania's eastern coast, to the place where our journey had found its beginning—Dar Es Salaam. The city looked just like we had left it. The crowded, bustling streets were alive. The frantic pedestrians and street beggars were in full movement. The jammed traffic lanes and blaring car horns were all cradled by the sounds of mosques throughout the city.

A New Path

After traveling to Mozambique, our small team said good-bye to one another. Randi would be staying in Mozambique. Nate would be heading to Tanzania. I would be on my way on a new path toward Russia, meeting up with a new team to travel there. Randi and I would meet back up in France a few months later to minister and continue our journey.

Suddenly, I was with a new team on a new path. I would team up with Paul and Josh, two extraordinary missionary guys who would be brothers for me along the way. We were on our way to Russia and landed in Tanzania's east coast to retrieve a visa for Russia at the local Russian embassy.

The embassy looked like it had been preserved in time. As we tiptoed into the black booth, an official equipped with a matching pair of thick black eyeglasses stared at us blankly. Hours later—and after several interrogation sessions, may I add—we were met with the devastating news that our request for a visa into Russia had been denied.

We weren't the kind of people to be easily swayed from our course, at least at this point in our travels. This was a normal occurrence in the life we had chosen. We had the option to quit or to get creative. We chose the latter. Hours later, we hopped a bus, going 15 hours through Tanzania back to Nairobi, Kenya. It was the coldest city I have visited in Africa. Our breath was visible and our tropical wardrobe and lack of winter apparel were an ironic statement in the midst of the frigid city breeze.

After being denied again in Kenya, we planned to hop a red-eye flight to London, England, to attempt one last time to get a visa into Russia. God had called us—we knew that much. But before we would, in fact, get that gift we had been searching for, life would spin in a direction we had never expected. The embodiment of the cost of following the voice of God would come in a package unforeseen and unexpected.

An Unexpected Expense

Walking back from the Internet café in Nairobi, I wondered if we were ever going to get to Russia. I was about a block away from our hostel as the late afternoon sun shone through the buildings around me.

I can still be swept up within the complexity of life that day. I could hear the sounds of horns blowing and traffic jams that occurred every day, yet oddly enough, those involved would seem just as shocked each day they found themselves within the trap.

I remember the sand and dirt blowing across my face as Nairobi's winter wind rippled through my jacket. It was cold this time of year. I could see snowflakes or at least icy rain falling on my flip-flops in front of me. It was an oxymoron, it seemed, to experience freezing temperatures in Africa. I laughed as I thought about the journey thus far to a nation we had never seen. Russia had proven to be the toughest and most closed door we had ever encountered. Feeling thoughts of defeat coming to my mind, I decided to throw them out the door and instead focus on the hot shower that would, in one moment, turn a day that had been sheer torture into a paradise full of bliss. It's so funny how the small things, when withheld, can seem like such treasures.

Rounding the corner, I could see the building we called home this week. Crossing the road, I felt that much closer to the showery reward that lay ahead. "It will all be worth it," I assured myself.

I walked into our hostel and the manager handed me our room key, attached to a large wooden block. Now, only three flights of steps kept me from a restful evening before friends who were traveling with me would return.

The steps were high and steep. As I rounded the first corner, a dark flash seemed to creep behind my right shoulder. I looked behind me but saw nothing. I must be paranoid. I was home. "Just a few more steps," I encouraged myself.

Running soon turned to small skips toward the end of the stairs. As I hit the landing, I could see our door in sight. A sense of relief came over me as I imagined rest that was well-needed. We had been traveling for over three years now. It was about time.

Then I heard them.

Behind me were footsteps. At first, slow. "Not a big deal," I thought. I continued for my door. As I inched nearer, the footsteps behind me came closer and faster. As my heart began to pound, I remembered a prank that Josh and Paul had done the day before, running after me and trying to kick in the door as typical brother types tend to do.

"It must be them," I thought. Yet in my conclusions, I couldn't look back. Only a couple seconds had gone by. I reached my key in the lock and turned it quickly to reach safety. "It will all be OK," I told myself as the open door felt like freedom.

It wouldn't be.

This day would be one that would shake my life to the core. The footsteps behind me would turn into hands around my throat. A thick, sharp knife blade pressed against my neck. I was pushed into our room. But this time, I would not be alone.

For what seemed like an eternity, I would be trapped. In an effort to not be killed, I fought back in segments, and soon my small limbs couldn't keep up.

In the minutes or hours that followed, I would be attacked and raped. Staring up at the small window covered with bars in the cement bathroom, I realized where I now would be imprisoned for longer than I could then imagine. My life had changed in an instant.

Later, alone yet lucky to be alive, I curled up in the corner. I knew that this attack would take me out of the lifestyle I had chosen for a long time. It could possibly be forever. I was shocked, alone, and in immense pain. What could I do? What now? Maybe I hoped I would wake up and it would all be a dream. As I opened my eyes, I realized that this was real life.

God provided the visas to Russia, and we went there directly following my attack. We continued ministering, teaching at an undercover school of missions near the Black Sea. I saw pain there, and I understood it. I also saw an overwhelming dependence on God, and I had known that, too.

I had been in Russia for a couple months and had encountered people whose lives mirrored chaos and passion like I had never before witnessed. My new friends knew what it was like to lose everything—to enter naked into the Kingdom of Heaven. They knew suffering on a degree that I could not fathom. But the look in their eyes startled me. They each carried faces of gentleness and resolve—childlike expectancy beyond the trauma they had known. Their God was real, and He always came running when they needed Him near.

But now God said it was time to go home.

So began my year of hiatus.

The Hidden Years

In Egypt, Mary's dream was *paused* as well. It was hidden. There was no glitz and glitter in carrying the Son of God in a dangerous place. National threats deported the young family to Africa. Death was lurking around an unfamiliar corner.

What was Mary thinking? Were fear, confusion, and questioning God's promise and protection in her thoughts? Where was God in the midst of this? It most definitely did not make sense in her mind. And now they were being hunted in a nationwide attempt at their lives and the life of their new baby. What do you do when your promise is threatened? What happens when our promise is put on hold? The *pause*. That pause is where Mary now found herself.

Mary, Joe, and Jesus could have spent up to ten years in Egypt.[3] The very word *Egypt* speaks of mystery. As refugees, Mary and her young family had to start a new life in a foreign land. They had no grasp of what this meant—no stability. Everything was new around them. This was the beginning of the hidden years.

She had been told on a moment's notice to leave everything she was behind. All that she had known, invested her life into, dreamed up, worked for—she was told to throw it away and run. Her old identity was shattered. Who was she supposed to be in a place she had never been to before?

Never mind the conflict she would have felt in leaving her family and her entire life behind. There was a direct attempt at her life and the breath of her promise. She had not been guaranteed safety. She had been asked to respond to providence, not circumstance.

These next years would not be full of acceleration and grandeur, but hiddenness, stillness, and waiting. Mary's promise would not be put on display for the whole world to see and take notice. It would be underground for the first few years of developing. Jesus would grow up in the shadows, unseen and tucked away from the rest of humanity. Mary's promise would be disguised until it was ready to be introduced to the public around them.

She would have to be forever on guard, watching over what had been spoken to her in the beginning. Her hiding place would be a refuge in the midst of extreme risk. What were Mary's thoughts while in hiding? What was going through her mind as she hid under cover?

The formative years of her promise would be in secret. Jesus would learn to walk in exile. He would learn His first words in the African dirt. He would learn all of these lessons from the lens on the margins. It was in exile where her promise would grow into fullness.

What would have happened if Mary had stayed in the spotlight once her destiny was birthed into the world? The development of her dreams would have come from a completely different realm. Why would God send a new movement of Heaven from the sidelines and the borders—the margins? What is it about God that He would choose the poor to bring forth palaces in the dust? Mary's pause in adversity would last for years.

Did you notice that Mary's destiny did not come in the form of a mature king equipped with royal robes and a golden rattle? It came as an immature, weak baby! The birthing of her promise would only be the beginning. What would come next—the hidden years—would be the true test of Mary's "yes."

When our promise is put on hold and when what we have been created to live in is in its beginning stages, we can get impatient. When our promise is threatened, we can become fearful and hide. There is a big difference between taking refuge in Heaven's shadow and running away in doubt and confusion. This pause is a chance for us to grow alongside our promise, one day at a time. It is an opportunity to rekindle our awareness of just how dependent we are, and for us to see our reflection in the mirror of our dream.

Knowing Our Need

Mary in all her natural mothering capabilities could not lift up her promise. She needed help, too! These hidden years were not a time for Mary to "suck it up" and become the "mommy of the year." These were the times for her to become transparent and come face to face with herself. These days would be a window for God to take over—times for Heaven to come close and couple with Mary's weakness and need.

Do we know our spiritual need? We cannot make our promise come forth in strength. We cannot lift ourselves or what we have been given up from the dust. We cannot do it on our own.

Why were Mary and her promise not rescued? In my journey, a constant piece of advice that people would give me was, "Jess, don't ask the 'why' questions. They'll only get you down." Now, experiencing what I have, I would have to disagree. God is OK with us wrestling with the hard questions of life. That doesn't always mean we will get a clear answer, but it does mean that He will stick with us in all of it.

Where I come from, the general answer to trauma is to get a "stiff upper lip" and to deal with it privately. In public, don't show your weakness—don't let your fragility be known and seen. If people knew who you really were, they wouldn't stick around, right? Be brave, be strong, and all that jazz.

The truth is that it's OK to be weak! When life comes crashing down around us, we can choose to feel it or to block it. In the end, we have to understand this reality.

Becoming People of the Tent

Jesus showed us the way to go. He left glory for the dirt! Before each of us is a choice to leave all we have known before and go follow Jesus into a Kingdom completely foreign to what we have lived in. This call to leave all—to leave country, family, everything that we have known and to press on—is not new. We find it even before Jesus showed up on the world scene, in the Abrahamic call.

Abraham and Sarah were called to a life outside of the borders. They were simply told to leave everything they had known before and to follow with no vision for what would happen. All Abraham was shown were the stars of the sky and a promise of children that would outnumber those twinkling balls of fire.

What would have happened if they had said "no"? We, too, have that choice. Trust me, trying to create your own promise is much harder than saying "yes" to what you have been created for. What we can produce in our own strength is a generic form of what we have been meant to be. And let's face it—generic formulas simply don't measure up to the real deal.

We have been asked to leave our identities that find themselves at odds with who we have been called out to become in the earth around us. Leaving all of our identities to find who we really are—*Whose* we are.

Giving our allegiance to the Kingdom of God means that we renounce our allegiance to anything else. Who are we when we take off the makeup that has been smeared on us by our identity in our family, our nations, our clubs, or our circles of friends? Giving everything over to Heaven means we let go of the reins and stick around for the ride, sometimes not knowing where we are headed, but trusting every inch of the way. We were created to leave everything behind for the sake of a new land—a homeland that we will come to find is our very own. We are to be "people of the tent."[4]

Who are the people of the tent? Following Jesus as spiritual nomads, they are those who are willing to go anywhere and leave anything to find Him. This is not merely for the single folks out there with nothing else better to do. Can you do this with a family? Abraham and Sarah did. Mary and Joe did. How are we any different?

"The Church is mission." My friend Lesley-Anne Leighton says this in hilarity. "Many people view [local or global] missions work today as single women with hairy legs in mud huts."[5] The paradigm for mission work—living in an outrageous relationship with God—in our day is changing. This is not a call to the few radical ones who cannot function in the Western church community. This is a call for the nations. Will we lay down all that we are for a dying world?

The face of missions—living our lives with Heaven in mind—is changing. In this day in mission efforts, more missionaries are being sent from the two-thirds world than from the first world. Countries all over Africa and other third world nations are sending forth missionaries who are bringing the Gospel to the Western world in word and demonstration of the power of the Holy Spirit.

The young are being called. But just as Elizabeth was pregnant with promise alongside Mary, so God is calling the old in our day. We need everyone who is living and breathing to join together in this movement.

Our picture of Jesus is also changing. More and more of us are waking up to the fact that we have bought into a false marketing campaign of faith. In its place is being erected a King in the dust—a Rogue who teaches us the upside-down way to go.

Living in Obscurity

Living in a place of attack. What happens when we have to sit down through the storm? Jesus slept through a storm while others panicked in fear. What happens in this time? What manifests as the good, the bad, and the ugly part of it all?

Living in a place of obscurity shows us just how powerful God is, letting us view life from a place of neediness. It is a place where we're doomed without Him. It is a seat where we begin to grapple with the reality that we cannot do anything to calm a storm, turn the tide, or turn back time. It is a location of coming face to face with our need.

Running away from our feelings, our questions, and our weakness can only extend this season. Mary could only run so far. Egypt would not give her an option to leave. If she did, her promise would surely die. Mary obeyed for the longevity of her promise. She knew what it was like to see her dream from its conception to its arrival. She also knew she had a long way to go, and the only way to see it through to fruition was to push through and accept this pause she found herself in the middle of.

When our life pauses, when our promise has been put on hold, what do we need? What did Mary do? She went on with life as usual. She continued to be a mother, just in a completely different place. When we learn to live in our promise no matter what location we find ourselves in emotionally, spiritually, physically, or geographically, nothing will be delayed in the embodiments of our dreams.

Great Expectations

Did Mary have an idea of what her promise would look like? In her expectancy, what would she have imagined? We all have preconceived ideas of what our futures will resemble. What had she dreamt up? If an angel showed up in your bedroom one night and told you God was going to use you to usher in the most outrageous move of God that would crash the earth and that you were going to birth a King whose throne would never end, what would you visualize that looking like? The last thing I would picture would be a filthy livestock shed as His first nursery, being deported and getting kicked out of the country, and nearly being killed.

It didn't look anything like she had planned. In fact, most of her life it would be very upside down. What comes to mind when you picture your destiny, your reason, and your promise? What will it look like? How will it come about? Have you dreamt of it? What do you see?

That is the nature of carrying Heaven. It will hurt. There will be deep and sometimes unsettling and unanswered questions. What kept Mary going? Could it have been those ponderings that she treasured? She would chew constantly on the words that had been spoken to her. The encounter that she treasured up within her heart—the visitation and overshadowing that would mark her forever—would continue to be relived.

We often have an idea of what our dreams or promises look like. They don't always go as planned. But God tends to use the unlikely to reveal His face.

Endnotes

1. Dr. Heidi G. Baker, director, Iris Ministries, Inc., www.iris-min.org.

2. Ibid.

3. George A. Buttrick, ed., *The Interpreter's Bible* (New York, NY: Abingdon Press, 1982).

4. Lesley-Anne Leighton, Director, Holy Given International School of Missions, www.holygiven.org.

5. Ibid.

Chapter 8

When the Promise Dies

He raises the poor from the dust and lifts the needy from the ash heap; He seats them with princes and has them inherit a throne of honor... (1 Samuel 2:8).

We were never guaranteed a life of ease when following in the footsteps of Jesus. At times, not being made aware of that from the beginning can send our systems into extreme shock once we encounter the devastating reality of this walk in our own lives.

Modern-day marketing has taken our imaginations captive, not to mention our minds, for that matter. We now know that with a little emotionally charged music, creative acting, and proper lighting and ambiance we can capture the world's complete attention. Something that at first glance is bland and plain can be transformed into a product with high demand.

Our society has grabbed our imaginations and pulled on the strings placed around us for one purpose—sell ability.

Sometimes we sell people catchy ideas—jingles of what it would look like to throw our lives away and trust God to show us which direction to go each step of the way. A life of outrageous interaction with Heaven becomes romanticized and beautified to a point where our "makeup" covers up the imperfections that we desire so strongly to mask. After all, we would never want to buy something that would continue to cost us, right? Some of that candid ability is creativity, which in its naked form is good. But false advertising gets us in big trouble once the "honeymoon" phase of following after Jesus fades away.

Imagine if someone divulged to you days before you were getting married that the "hitched" lifestyle was full of candy hearts, chocolate-covered strawberries, and heartfelt serenades. Envision the "big picture" that you are handed, nothing less than a Norman Rockwell clone—smiles, googly eyes, and sheer, uninterrupted bliss. The honeymoon never ends. Or does it?

Every little girl dreams, from the moment she sees her first wedding in real life or in play, of herself in a white dress one day. Make-believe soon becomes immersed in colors, flowers, dancing, and the lipstick of the "big day." All eyes are on her, and they live "happily ever after" *blah blah blah.* That is what we ladies daydream about from toddlerhood to the day we skip down the aisle to our "prince" who is waiting for only us. Yet most of us will never let ourselves think past those famous words of "I do" to the following week, when there's nothing around but messy dishes, irking behaviors by our significant other that drive us up the wall, and a filthy house to be cleaned.

Most of us in no way think about the underside of the vows we commit to in front of our families and all of Heaven. Think about those vows of sticking through it all together—through poverty and wealth, through sickness and in health, through tragedy and miracles, through love and hate. Our culture shows that when push comes to shove, people will leave and quit when "the going gets tough." We run from suffering, tests, and trials. We not only hide, but we make excuses for the rationale of throwing in the towel. We stand up for our rights, and our words that echo through time, from the moment of that covenant to now, are swept under the rug. We declare they no longer carry any value. We void our promises.

When we decide to give our lives to Jesus, we lay down our rights. We choose to exchange our promises for His. The promises He gives us will never disintegrate, but will remain through tough and easy times.

Saying "yes" to His cup means a marriage, a merger of these opposites. Those divergent realities are love and pain, suffering and joy, and tears and laughter. We may not be able to understand why these happen, but Jesus gives us freedom to ask the hard questions, to wrestle through the rough times, and to participate in healing even in our own lives. This wrestling is where Jesus meets with us face to face.

Heaven's Melody

Underneath the tent, life was in full swing. The air around us was dancing with sand flying in every direction. The ancient keyboard that we used to produce any beat possible was louder than I remembered. I felt like I was in the middle of a cardio workout video.

Children covered in mud and sand surrounded me. My hands were joined with theirs, and every fabric of my being was caught up in this one moment. It was as if life stood in slow motion before me. Their smiles were engraving themselves in my memory. Their little shrieks of laughter and giggles carried a melody that I catch myself singing every day without knowing it.

Sweat became a magnet for dirt. I looked down at my feet and noticed a very defined "tan" line, which was really a masterpiece of sand, sweat, and bugs. When I looked up, I caught a glimpse of pure joy. This place had become part of who I was. I was home…and knew I never wanted to leave.

A Strange Land

Suddenly, I was jolted and awakened by the loud intercom of the airplane pilot. "Ladies and gentlemen, on behalf of our airways I would like to welcome you to John F. Kennedy airport. Have a great day here in the New York area or wherever your destination may take you."

Groggy from jet lag, I remembered where I now found myself. I was in North America again. Africa was now an ocean of water away, and the children I had just been dancing with were mere memories and dreams. I was "home." But I felt more foreign in this land than in any other I had entered.

The last three and a half years, I had found myself in countries around the world, learning and living with the poor. I had learned to love and be loved in the midst of simplicity, war, poverty, death, and family. Somehow it all came to a sudden pause. And that pause would prove to be one of the greatest journeys of my life.

The Pause

I didn't fit in. I didn't even know how to function in the life I used to know. After a few months of preaching, things slowed down.

I missed my life. I mourned the dreams I had known as reality before. I longed for the hunger and the look in the eyes of a child who knew the fullness of suffering and joy.

It was as if someone shoved me under water and told me to breathe deeply. I honestly felt like I was dying. Sound familiar? I always thought that giving our lives away for Jesus was a very mystical and powerful decision, and it is. What no one ever told me was that those pauses in our lives are some of the deepest valleys we can experience. It is in those places and times where we can either lose or win. For me, this pause would prove to be a journey of deep mourning and great joy.

Me? I fought this season. And trust me, I fought with all that I had in me. At first, my heart trusted God on being away from the land I knew I was called to. I pressed into His presence. After all, it was the only real thing I had left.

Most people looked at me with confused faces when I told them of blind eyes seeing and the Kingdom of God falling among the poor. To deal with the pain in my own life, I had filled every moment with keeping busy. I took heavy course loads to finish a degree at a conservative Christian university, and actually had a professor who would call me out and tell the class that I was delusional for believing that God still spoke with people in our day. In his teachings, God couldn't possibly heal or work in the ways He had always said He would do. Looking around me, I saw classes of students who were headed for dead-end roads with a vision of buildings, numbers, and dependence on their own strengths and charismatic personalities.

Suddenly, life became complicated, and I wasn't sure how to go about the road that was now in front of me. I was used to seeing Jesus in one form—in the eyes of the world's poor. I would have to learn to see Him in the midst of many disguises.

Candy-Coated Love

So now on to the underside, this place that I gave you a glimpse of in the beginning. What is the underside? And how can we experience God's presence in the midst of it? The low end of a life laid down for love looks anything but glamorous and beautiful. Underneath the miracles and the invasion of Heaven coming to the earth, there is a cost—a cause and effect relationship.

Does saying "yes" to God's intentions for your life mean that you will experience extreme situations like I have or like those around the world? It might not look the same, but I simply do not want to candy-coat the truth for you. A life like this—living in radical relationship with God, whether you are a missionary in the slums of India or a businessman in the corner office in New York City—will cost you something. The more you say "yes," the more expensive your price tag will be.

A life thrown away for Love Himself is not just for the radicals who run to the war zones of the world and sell everything they have to follow Jesus. This is for anyone who wants to know the reality of God in his midst, Jesus in him, the power that can turn the world, the financial markets, and the systems all on their heads.

Heaven is ushering in a final wave of those who will give everything for Love's sake. This will mean much more than forfeiting mere material possessions and goods. It will be much pricier than giving up your goals or ambitions for success. For some, it will cost us our lives.

Those who followed Jesus were never accepted by society—rarely at best. The original handful all died at the hands of those they came to serve, just as Jesus did. For all of us, the cost will be different. But there will be a cost.

Centering too much on either side of the proverbial fence of the Kingdom of God gets us into trouble. We will talk about more of this later, but the underside is also only part of what our journey will look like. Are we supposed to stay there? We were created, ironically, to live in the cohesive relationship of the good and the hard side of love. Fashioned to live in the hard times and the bad. Suffering and joy that grip us with equal measures of force.

How do we live in the reality of a marriage of polar opposites? When we begin living from the lens of knowing what Heaven thinks of us, our lives take on an entirely different spin. This cause-and-effect relationship in our lives carries with it gifts. When we encounter suffering, God gives us joy that strengthens us if we accept it. When we mourn and weep, He gives us laughter and dancing. When we make ourselves nothing, He raises us up farther than we could ever climb on our own.

Whether we say "yes" or "no" to God's promises in our lives, we will face heartache, stress, and a multitude of other traumas. Have you ever looked into the eyes of the seemingly "successful" in our day? What do you see?

Do you see anguish and pain, frustration, and constant worry about keeping themselves where they have risen to? If life is based on own ability and strength, like it or not, eventually what we have built will crumble at our feet anyway.

The difference between a life given over to God and one driven on its own will is the effect—the end result. We will all have suffering and pain. Only when we yield to Heaven's cooling rain can we receive what we need in the midst of that. Joy for sadness. Laughter for weeping. Dancing for depression. Healing for sickness. Love for hate. It becomes upside down. It's our choice, though, to stand on our heads. The question for all of us is—are we willing to go through the back door, the underside, to get to the glory, miracles, hope, and freedom? Only those who have known bondage can take captivity captive. We can only give what we have been given. What do you have to give? Our greatest pain often becomes our greatest strength and victory.

When we choose to join those on the margins, when we can see from the perspective of those we serve, when we sit in the dust with the lowly, we finally see ourselves for who we really are—equals in the same boat of need. Living a missional lifestyle—a life of joining with God's heart in the world around us—can be completely different than most of us have signed up for. When we consistently find ourselves on the high end, the end of dominance and strength, we miss the posture of Jesus. Even as King, He made Himself low, even sinking to the level of the prostitutes, the hated, the shunned, and the untouchables. Think about it. He came through a poor girl in the sand. Why would Heaven do that?

When Darkness Falls

Everything in my life suddenly stopped. The only thing around me that remained was silence. I felt alone. There was no gold dust, feathers, or other supernatural paraphernalia for me to relish in. In my head, my promise was dead and was never coming back.

Living in the death of our promise is a crazy predicament to be in. How do we go on living in strength when what is inside of us feels dead? Some of us can choose another plan, another route, and another "great life plan." I couldn't. For me, there had never been a plan B. I dove into what God had put inside of me at an age when I didn't have enough sense to think any differently, thank goodness!

Imagine being on a long journey, and in the middle of your adventure, your odyssey takes you to a cliff. The road is invisible or absent, depending on what you trust and believe. There is nothing in front of you—no bridge, no way out. You've gone too far to go back. What do you do?

My identity was depleted…at least, I thought so. This place of emptiness is where we can be reawakened to finding our true identity. Do you know who you are? If we strip ourselves of our crutches in life for self-fulfillment, what are we left with? And are we OK in that naked, uncovered, transparent state?

Of course not! At least, I wasn't. I'd like to tell you that I got up, dusted the dirt off my knees, and kept going. But life isn't like a sporting game. I couldn't just smile and fake it until I made it. That wouldn't work anymore. I had to face the ugliness in my life head-on if I ever wanted to go on.

What did I feel like? I felt like everything I had ever worked for was ripped into shreds, distorted, and broken beyond repair. Suddenly the journey that I was on seemed more like a mean joke from God than a precious gift.

I remember feeling so angry toward God one day. Why would He give me something so beautiful, a dream to change the world, and then sit back as it was snatched away?

I found my Bible and journal. Staring down at the pages, I realized I hadn't been able to write in over six months. In frustration, I ran to the kitchen and stuffed the two books in the trash. It was my meager attempt at "getting even." I was out of ideas!

Have you ever been in that situation? A place that is so incredibly uncertain and empty that any action seems better than nothing, even if it is in a negative reaction? This might shock you, but I'm pretty sure that, when I tossed my Bible and writings into the garbage, Jesus giggled. Some of you are about to hurl this book in the rubbish heap reading this, but whether it busts open your theological boxes or not, God loved me more in that moment of complete honesty and weakness than all of the times where I worked to "get life right." He was OK with my openness and my hurt. He could handle it! Even in my hurt, I must have sensed that. The Bible and journals did not stay in the trash.

How did I continue? I honestly didn't at times. I tried what most people do. I made myself extremely busy. And by busy I mean I worked three jobs and went to school for a degree, taking more than double of the allotted hours students could take. I was basically immersing myself within one-hundred-hour weeks. It was my attempt at hiding. And, if I'm candid, it did work for a while—but nothing that is generic lasts forever.

When the Promise Flatlines

Jesus was suffering. Mary's dream was being seemingly destroyed. What was she feeling as she watched her promise slowly being crushed? Did she feel helpless? Hopeless? How would she hold on for dear life?

Life had gotten steady, and she had grown older. In her heart, she still felt like the little teenager whose life had been wrecked beyond all recognition. It had been over three decades, and yet the promise that was before her still had not come to fruition. She wondered why it had taken so long.

Mary was a contemplative—a mystic who treasured in her heart all that had been whispered in her ears the night that Heaven invaded her little life. Now, 30-some years later, she thought she had faced all the struggling and suffering that the world had to offer. After all, she had encountered some of the most extreme situations just by agreeing to go along with this outrageously awkward celestial game plan.

As a young woman, the controversy that ensued after her initial encounter multiplied as the days went by. Some people around her would leave. Others would look down on her in disgust and dismay. Only a few would remain at her side. She left everything for Love's sake. What a real-life version of "love at first sight"!

She could see it all again. The crowded barn was dripping with residue of the rain that had blanketed the fields the night before. Her promise lay embodied in her arms. This was her life! In those small and fleeting moments, life seemed perfect, whole, and safe. It wouldn't stay that way for long.

Now, Mary was older. The ups and downs of the unmarked road she had come through thus far were behind her. She had made it through. Yet soon would come another trial, one that was not a part of the divine announcement she had been given so many years ago.

Suddenly a voice barged in through her door uninvited. It was her son's friends. "Jesus has been arrested!" They shouted, out of breath.

"What? Arrested? Why?" Mary panicked and ran to the city interior.

Lies were being shouted against her promise. Jesus remained silent—He wouldn't speak a word to defend Himself. Looking at her son, she wanted to scream and protect the one God had given her. As the guards beat Him beyond recognition, tears ran down Mary's aged cheeks. She was clueless of what to do, but her heart was breaking in helplessness. What *could* she do? She was supposed to protect her promise, wasn't she? But how could she?

The very gift she had been given was breaking in front of her. All she could do was wait. As the city streets crowded with bloodthirsty gangs of people, the words echoed forever in her memory. "Kill him!" Again and again the sentence rang through the air.

Her promise was being mocked in front of her. What exactly was Mary feeling as she watched her gift, her destiny, being crushed? God had pledged that He would be King. Yet all she could see was a homeless son who was charged as a traitor—who hung with the most unattractive and unwanted of society.

As Jesus hung on a splintered piece of wood, tears of defeat fell from Mary's cheeks to the ground. As she sobbed, her veil was whipping in the Israeli wind. "It's over," she thought. Her everything was gone. Was she just supposed to "get over it" and leave? How could she go on with life? He *was* her life!

Mary sat at the foot of the Cross and wept in a heap of sorrow. Her promise was dead—a death she had encountered alongside Him. The angel had not told her this would happen, that this tragedy would also be a part of her story.

Was she angry? "You promised me!" she might have shouted upward toward Heaven. She had given her life to birth and bring up Heaven's Son. It had cost her all she had. She gave up everything. Was *this* how it all would end? Had God lied to her?

Anger transitioned to weakness and confusion. "Why?" Mary whispered as she fell to the ground, unable to get back up. What happens when accusations come against what God has placed inside of us? When lies were being shouted against Mary's hope, what did she do? There will be times when all hell will come against the words given to us—against our promise. A lot of times, this attack will come in the form of questions—incriminating thoughts and words that question the nature and expectation of what has been spoken to us.

Mary had birthed a new movement of God in the earth around her. She had nurtured it, protected it, and sacrificed for its well-being. The angel had blatantly told her she would carry a ruler, the King who would reign over all of both Heaven and earth. The very name of her promise—the title that He carried—was attacked and called into question.

"Are you the King of the Jews?" they shouted in mocking laughs. In the chaos that pummeled Mary's ears, she would have to choose to listen beyond the crowd's lies. She would have to push through what was in front of her and find the truth. Mary would have to remember her promise—her words of hope in their raw, untainted format.

What has God spoken to you? What is inside of you? You get just this one shot. Don't let it pass you by. No matter what the cost is, run with it. When it seems to crumble at your feet, remember. That remembering will help you hold on for dear life.

Turned Upside Down

My world had been turned upside down. When our promise is being crushed in front of us—threatened and torn apart—we have a choice. We can believe what has been told to us by Heaven or we can believe lies that come against our hope.

In my own life, that has been easier said than done. There were days when I watched what was inside of me fade and seem like it was taking its last breaths, never to move again. I didn't always choose to believe what God had spoken to me. I didn't always trust Him at His word. No amount of miracles can prepare us for trials and suffering. When those times hit us, they can shake us to the very core of who we are.

There are days in my life that, when all else fails, I stick Post-it notes on my bathroom mirror. I put reminders all around me to evoke memories of what God originally said to me.

We need to do whatever it takes to store these promises within our hearts. How do we remember and hold on when what is around seems to solidify the death of what we have been told—the massacre of what we have given our lives for?

Some say, "What we behold, we become." I think that is true, but more so—who we dwell on, we truly transform into being. There are things we can do to remember the promises that God has placed within us. Placing our promise before our eyes day and night can help. Ultimately though,

Jesus is the only One who can bring lasting life to something that is dead. He is the One we need to stick close to. In His eyes, new life will come.

When our promise is besieged and stolen, we can react in a few different ways. We can hide and run from what is happening. We can shut down and give up. Or we can face it head-on and stick through to the other side, not knowing what will happen.

I acted out all of these scenarios until I finally found what I needed. Graham Cooke says, "Environment is key to development." When we are floundering, hiding only prolongs the process of healing.[1] We need to find others who are struggling, too—a community that is set on recovering together in openness and transparency.

Environment is key! I had to travel even farther to get somewhere like that. I'll share that story with you in the next chapter, but until then, know that our promise—whether in death or life—was never meant to be experienced alone. Heaven surrounds us and gives us others who walk the journey with us, even carrying us at times when we can't lift ourselves from the dust.

Loving in the Midst of Hatred

Mother Teresa said, "I have found the paradox, that if you love until it hurts, there can be no more hurt, only more love."[2] To me, every person in front of me—including the one in the mirror—is in need and spiritually poor. We can love until we turn blue in the face. Only when we love regardless of the consequence can we step forward on the road in front of us.

I asked myself many questions during my year of hiddenness. I wondered—am I willing to love in the midst of hatred? Is love a mere theory of thought, or is it truth? Does it suffer long? Does it really never fail? Webster's Dictionary cannot even define love as a tangible action. We've watered it down so much that none of us can really describe what it entails.

173

Incarnational love is a choice to be Jesus in a culture. It is about loving in the midst of injustice. We come as learners, just as He did. We sit with the people, learn their needs, and serve them for the destiny of their people group. Jesus has placed Himself in our hands.

How do we love in the face of hatred? That is a question with an answer that I am still learning to this day. I still have a difficult time loving a person who cuts me off in traffic! Deciding to live a lifestyle of love means that we love regardless of the result of the exchange. It means that we give everything, sometimes knowing we will be left with nothing.

Letting Go

Letting go of our promise takes every ounce of strength we can muster. Relinquishing control seems impossible when it comes to something we have given everything for. Becoming dependent and childlike again when we've thought that we learned it all seems redundant and even rude, don't you think?

Trusting even when what we have been given is taken away—believing even when our promise is missing and nowhere to be found—is one of the hardest situations we can face in the wake of watching our dreams being crushed in front of us. Jesus promised us that, *"You're blessed when you feel you've lost what is most dear to you. Only then can you be embraced by the One most dear to you"* (Matt. 5:4).

Lose Your Life

After throwing our lives away for God, we have a chance to say "yes" again when our promise is stolen or attacked. To be overshadowed again. God can make all things new. He can resurrect the deadest of things!

It doesn't mean we are to trust blindly, though. It's OK to wrestle; it's OK to be honest about where we are. Quickly saying "yes" again and having deep-seated, concealed hurts and pains can only lead to a harder and more devastating crash later. We have to deal with what is inside of us. We cannot dismiss it, but need to face it head-on.

Will you give your life away? What does that even look like? When the fairy-tale portion is peeled away, those questions can cripple us. It doesn't mean you have to sell all that you have and move to a walled city in China, though for you, it might. Dig deep and look again inside yourself.

What has God shown you? Can you remember the whispers given to you from Heaven? What is inside of you? Forget the voices in your head that say your promise is dead. What have you been promised?

Put it in front of yourself once more. Do you know your promise? Do you believe that, even when the pulse is flatlined, life can burst in? When we choose to put our hope in the One who is life instead of our own useless strength, a miracle greater than any other can take place before our eyes.

Handpicked

There is no one God does not want. When God looked down on the earth, He saw Mary—a young girl in the Israeli dust, just minding her own business. There she was, in her ordinary life setting, not looking for life to look any differently, and Heaven broke into her life. God put His finger on Mary, and her life would never look the same again.

God wants you! Not simply for what you can do. That doesn't really matter anyway! He could do it all Himself if He wanted. But He *chooses* you. When He looks down in our day and sees you in your day-to-day life, you ravish His heart. One touch from Heaven and your world will be turned upside down.

You've been handpicked by Heaven to carry its nature. Sure, the road is going to be rough, bumpy, and long. Along the way, there will also be wonders that you could only imagine and times when Jesus will show up, if only to remind you He has been there the entire time.

Participating in the Kingdom of Heaven has very little to do with our strength. If anything, we qualify by our weaknesses. There are no tryouts in a life of giving everything over to God. You don't have to audition for the part. The part has been designed around who you are and *who* He sees you as! You have been created to fill that role.

- Let's get one thing straight—God wants *you!* Being overshadowed by Heaven means that who you are becomes consumed by who He is. You were meant to live in Heaven's delight.

Endnotes

1. Graham Cooke, "The Way of the Warrior," http://direct.crossrhythms. co.uk/product/The-Way-Of-The-Warrior-1/Graham-Cooke/94329.

2. Mother Teresa, http://qutations.about.com/.

Chapter 9

Fight by Laying Down

"All that is not [fully] given is lost." —Indian Proverb

The greatest injustice that could happen within this road together is for you to receive a load of spiritual clichés that look great in your journal and on bumper stickers or T-shirts but cannot translate into real life. How useless and tragic would that be! Let's get up front and honest about the entire picture of love—the beautiful, the ugly, and the downright unbelievable facets of choosing to live life in this most scandalous of ways. It is the barebones reality of this lifestyle that we can choose to be a part of in our own existences.

Suffering is a beautiful and mysterious word until it becomes personal when its blunt force hits home. Sure it's bewitching on paper. But when all the makeup and lipstick is smeared off and only the raw, painful reality remains, it loses its luster. As an idea, we elevate it. As a way of life, we run from it or hide at best.

Grappling with our own upside-down, inside-out stories can be a draining metamorphosis. Coming to terms with the raw, disfigured facts that encompassed my own life was a long process. Lingering in a season of waiting was tough! To be made to rest is one of the most appalling suggestions I have ever encountered. It went against everything I had ever been taught! I just couldn't understand how suffering and joy could coexist together. The truth is, this inside-out Kingdom houses both.

When a storm—and by storm I mean a hijacking of our destinies— bombs our lives, life and death seem to exist on one level playing field. Remember the Israelites who followed Moses? Their compass was a cloud by day and a fire by night. (Pretty amazing GPS system, if you ask me!) That same cloud of God's presence still visits us to this day.

When the cloud of God's existence interrupts our lives, it doesn't look like what we might have imagined. The large, white, fluffy, marshmallow-like objects that resemble cotton balls more than actually clouds are nowhere to be found. Instead, many times this cloud hovering above us is dark, heavy, and about to burst over top of our little lives.

The cloud of God's glory brings life within it. When the storm hits, it brings the answer to our crisis. What to us looks like a looming path of destruction turns into an ironic twist of fate. It is a moment where God uses a storm to usher in a whirlwind of new life, sustenance, and refreshing rain.

When we get to this low place, yielding, letting God do His job, and laying down our rights,[1] healing can hit us like a sweeping wind. But in order for healing to come, it requires of us complete surrender.

No Cover Charge!

I can remember spending time with Talia along the road throughout Africa's plains. She knew utter devastation. She was homeless, family-less, and locked alone in a world of silence. Each day as I held her, she would kick, scream, and bite if need be to loose herself from the arms of love. Deep down, she craved it. But vulnerability was the blockade that kept her from its depths.

There was finally a day when my little friend yielded herself to love. A moment in time when the realization came—Love was free. The only way for her to fight was by laying down, allowing her wounds to be exposed, and jumping in, uncensored. I saw myself in her eyes in the instant when I was in the very shoes she was in—a little girl in a pair of small orange flip-flops.

Some of you have been hurt deeply in watching your promises struggle and fall limp before you. You wonder, "Where did it go?" As I write, I can even see those who have concluded that the days of their promise are behind them—that your time has "run out." There are some who feel profoundly jaded by the merger of opposites within their own lives and the seeming-broken contract that Heaven has made to them. What's more, many in this same position feel completely alone.

Have you felt the signs of life, the rhythm of Heaven within you? Can you remember what was promised to you by God? What did He place inside of you? Hold onto it. There will be seasons of death in our lives, and they are not fun! But you are not alone. And those seasons do not last! Death has to submit itself to Heaven's hand—life. Winter must turn to spring.

You have been created for more than a paycheck. You have been made for purpose—a plan that can only exist and flourish outside of yourself. If you feel barren and robbed of your God-given dream, you are in the right spot, and you are on the right track!

When our promise lies dead before us, what do we do in those moments when we stare silently, waiting for only a small sign of life—a glimmer of hope? What do we do in the waiting? These times can make or break us. There are a few options for us in these seasons. We can run from the carnage and pretend it never happened. We can try to forget and creatively make up another great life plan. Or we can wrestle with God in the waiting, in the why, and in the shock of the unexpected. The rebirth of our promise is also a choice we get to make that can only come from the window of waiting.

Seasons of waiting can also be intense periods of restoration and re-demption—times of healing. Seconds turning into hours can revive our hope one inch at a time. Many of us have been used to the rallying cry that says to "stand up and fight," "take the land," and all that hocus-pocus. In theory, that is a nifty motto. But in real life, I'm afraid it misses the potholes of our lives—the unexpected crashes that leave us immobile and helpless.

There are times in our lives when proactive fighting will get us nowhere. Instances when we have to realize and accept that we are handicapped in doing a job that can only be done by Heaven. Nights when our true battle will be won by lying down instead of rising up. Many of us have been taught to "fight for our rights," but I would encourage you to give your rights away, get on the ground, and use your resources. If Heaven is behind you, what more do you need?

Fight by laying down—what does that mean? Our greatest weapon of war in the Spirit does not mirror the natural realm. Sure, we all want to mimic William Wallace—the hero in the hit movie *Braveheart*—rallying the people to victory. We desire to be brave. We are told we must be in order to "make it," aren't we? The "do-it-yourself" version of healing doesn't always make the cut. In the instants when your promise is dead and part of you goes with it, there's only one action left to do—position yourself for what only Heaven can do.

That's just my point! We've been beckoned into a Kingdom that costs us nothing to reside in! A land where having nothing makes us rich, being weak makes us powerful, and being captive makes us free. It is a place for the broken to co-reign with the One who knows exactly what we are thinking in our need. A new home full of everything we could ever need, want, or imagine. It's not a fairy-tale realm, but more real than what we can touch with our hands.

A Broken Spirit

When our spirit or will gets broken, everything around us can seem to come to a halting stop. The "cloud" that hit my own life carried with it enough rain to flood my environment. My biggest struggle was learning and figuring out how to stay afloat when I felt as if I was drowning!

Even while writing about my life as I hit bottom, I felt stuck. In truth, I was. It was as if I was caught in a marsh of quicksand, and every movement I made attempting to free myself only forced me deeper into an internal prison of silence. I was utterly frustrated, exhausted from trying to fix myself, and confused at the 180-degree turn that my life had suddenly taken without my consent.

As odd as it sounds, there is magnificent power in being broken and *knowing* it. A broken life carries with it a melody. Our pain soon becomes our praise—the very place where we meet Jesus face to face for who He really is. In our lowest place and our darkest hour can come an awareness of destiny revealed. The reversal of fates where, when our promise seems impossible, God breaks in with His final chess move, and the underdog becomes the victor.

Looking down at photographs from the road I had been on, the previous years quickly turned from a time of laughter and reminiscence to sadness and perplexity. The smiles, the people, and the simple yet majestic way of life I had known all seemed to have been swallowed up by a cloud of despair. Gazing down at myself holding a little girl I had known, I wondered, "Was this my life?" It seemed so very foreign.

Life had taken a drastic turn, and the year that followed was met with fears and unknowns that I had never dreamt of. Deep within my heart, I knew who I was. I knew somewhere within me that my promise was still going to take a small breath, even if it were a quiet and unnoticeable gasp.

The year was full of deep-seated questions, and after awhile I had no choice but to be completely honest with God about *all* of them. There were many more than I had thought! Day in and day out, I wondered if I would ever get my life back. There were mornings that I can remember waking up and praying it was all a dream.

What did I feel? I felt empty and void. There were times when I was angry that it suddenly looked like God had lied and failed to keep His promise. Confusion as to the "whys" of it all engulfed my heart. Thinking back, that year was one of the most shaking times of my life.

In that survival mode is where I let myself collapse. Sure, it didn't look pretty from the outside. It can make things uncomfortable for those around you. And there are consequences to being vulnerable and transparent, even if it is just between you and Jesus. To others I looked a mess. To Heaven, I was right where I needed to be. The note to self was simple—let yourself fall. Fall to His feet.

At His Feet

The ride from Russia to France was bumpy. I was quite sick and can remember my face turning several shades of yellows and greens. While journaling I wrote, "A people called to His feet will find their home there."

It didn't matter what culture we were in. We all needed His presence. Without it, nothing else mattered. Paris carried a familiar spirit of dependence on God's presence. I looked around me, and a group of Arab youth lined the floor crying out to God. Randolph, a friend who ministers in a beautiful church in Paris, had invited us. It always amazed me how he would drop everything if Heaven would swarm in.

I couldn't believe that we had managed to find homes throughout the world. Each place we would visit housed a twin hunger and others that were on a similar pilgrimage. There on the floor we began to call out what we saw God doing in the lives of those around us.

It is in this place—this posture at the feet of Jesus—that we begin to tear down the hierarchal trends that we've set up. We start to break down the seats of status that we've built up for ourselves and others. And we take a plunge in realizing that all of us really are on the same level. Special ranking gets thrown out the window, and we catch ourselves side by side with everyone else who has come to the understanding of their own vast spiritual need.

When we are used to the position of being "on top" of the spiritual totem pole—when our habits generally place us on the dominant end, the affluent high chair—there is a crossing-over that has to take place. There is a piece within us that wants to change the world.

How do you love? Now, that's a hard question. Loving and giving of ourselves has first got to be about those we serve and not secretly for ourselves. There is a sense of prestige that goes along with those who help others—the "less fortunate," we call them. Though I am thankful for the swarms of people who give to the needy, the entire paradigm of this movement needs to shift.

We cannot approach a life given away for love in a manner that makes us (or keeps us) on the upward end, the dominant position, and if we are honest, the powerful level. The "haves" and the "have-nots" are separated immensely in the societies we live in. The transition that needs to take place is for us to step past the cultural lines that have been drawn. It is a joining of ourselves with those whom we serve. It is a merger of the margins. We immediately become a different caste.

A Season of Waiting

In a matter of hours, Mary's world had been turned upside down. What was going on? What was she feeling and struggling with? Was Mary's mind spinning? Was her heart breaking?

There is nothing written on Mary's three days of mourning. We do know that everyone around her fled—many went into hiding—and there was danger all around them. With so much fear to gather, was she alone? Mary was suddenly left with nothing, and everything was gone.

In less than 24 hours, her dream lay dead in front of her. She had given away her entire life to bring breath to a new movement only to see it crushed before her eyes. Over three long decades, she had worked.

"Was it all for nothing?" she wondered.

Let's pretend for a moment that Mary was a normal, small-town girl. (She actually was, just in case you were wondering!) She was pitched face-first into a battle where her hands were tied. There He was, her hope being broken before her. As she looked at Him, she could hardly recognize His face all bloodied and beaten. Why would God allow the very thing He gave as a gift to be thrown away? Yet Mary was chained—bound from being able to save her dream. She could do nothing but wait through the chaos that spun around her. She was heartbroken. Emotions flooded her body from all directions.

As darkness hit out of the blue that late afternoon, the lights went out in her own life. She watched her dream, her everything, take its last breath. There was nothing but silence and the sound of weeping coming from her own heart. Her promise was broken, but Mary was shattered along with it.

This made absolutely no sense! Why was this happening? Had God lost His mind? Had He lost? Or was He simply stoic and had disappeared? The darkness that hit that day would only be the beginning of yet another season for Mary—a period of intense waiting.

What happened in those next three days? What would you do when you see your promise die in front of your eyes? She had not been given anything but the end result and was asked to trust through all of the unknowns. But this was a *big* unknown!

Mary was asked to wait again. Could she continue to trust? She had to be prepared for her promise not to come back to her. She was asked to be willing to still obey even in confusion when she did not understand. Even when the unthinkable happened, would she say "yes"?

In the times of waiting in our own lives, our choice to say "yes" becomes even more vital. What did Mary do when the angel was no longer there to assure her of what would be? These times of seeming isolation in the death of our promises define us to the core. These are moments when we must choose to hold on to the echoes of the promises made to us so long ago. Mary treasured those vows in her heart. Could that have been what saw her through to the other side?

All That Is Not (Fully) Given Is Lost

In the mourning haze that I found myself in, I wondered, "Where is it?" Who are we when we are stripped of everything that defines us? What happens when all the bells and whistles that we use to justify our existence disappear before our eyes? Who are we anyway?

When the lights go down, there's only truth left to see. When the curtain goes back and nothing but the sounds of crickets remain, we are left with the shocking reality of who we are without all we've done to cover ourselves up. I would like to cut us some slack, however, because I know that in the Western world, society pretty much sets us up for failure in this realm. The harder we work, the harder we fall. In unspoken rules, we are taught to hide within our cliques, family, careers, and even our churches. There are not many safe places for us to be real with each other, are there? But that is what we so desperately need! Safe houses for those of us who are choosing to come out of hiding and into the light of exposure that is found in God alone.

I thought that I knew what it was to "give my life away"—to "give it up" completely and entirely. There was much more of me to lay down—a part of me that I really never knew existed.

Mary had to wait and linger for three days. My journey took over a year. I wrestled most of the way against the overwhelming conversion I found myself lost in. There was so much more I hadn't known—so much more to Heaven's reality that I had never before been taught.

Growing up in a small country town in the United States, suffering was, for the most part, a taboo word only to be mentioned under your breath. When a person went through hard times, the solution was always to cover it up behind closed doors, of course. Band-aids on open wounds and microwave "Mr. Fix-it" directions on the most raw of experiences just never made sense to me. Especially when I found myself on the other side of the tracks—the other side of the proverbial fence.

God wants all of us. He wants the good, the bad, and the ugliness of our lives. He wants our weakness, our joy, our tears, and our sadness. He wants it all! Are we willing to give Him everything?

A Gateway to Hope

Weeping and mourning are gateways to laughter and joy. Death can become the bridge to life. How upside down is that? When I was first posed with the very door that I've been writing about, I was scratching my head, too. I felt like Alice in Wonderland.

Do you remember her story? There she was, growing enormously and needing to go through a small, low door. The only way out was to get low—she had to become smaller. The land she was seeking after was so close to her that she could hear it as she pressed her ear against the thin wooden door. Through the low door was a kingdom she thought existed only in her dreams. When Alice figured out how to get to the low place, she was capable of entering into a realm beyond herself. It was the land that housed the answer to her longing, curiosity, and hunger.

Developing a posture that mimics the one Jesus took takes all of ourselves. There can be days where the destruction of our hearts can seem to overwhelm us to a point of paralysis. Times where nothing else can be in view, and life seems to be dwindling in front of us. But it doesn't end here! Many people stop just short of a breakthrough in their lives. Trust me, I've been there, too. The fact is, life will not stay that way. Change is always moving. Mourning the death of our promises will always turn to dancing in the renewal of what is inside of us...if we wait for the transformation to come. Though it takes time and though it lingers, wait for it. It will surely come.

A Turning Tide

I tried for months to figure out a new plan for my life. I listened to everyone for what I should be doing, all the while knowing deep within me that their plans were all bogus compared to what God had originally showed me.

The healing of the blind man in Mozambique showed me that sometimes healing is a process, one that can be equally as frustrating as it is breathtaking. Only something that is dead can be revived. And sometimes, in order for us to experience great power in our lives, we have to be willing to wrestle through great weakness.

Our greatest weakness can become our greatest source of strength. Our pain has a melody to it, and the dance and song that God gives us in its midst draws others to join in on the same. That sound is an anthem forming in the earth. A rallying cry that has existed since the dawn of time, waiting to be picked up by those willing to pay the price of carrying it.

An anthem is a unifying sound given to a group of people who join in one heart and mind. What is the song of your life? Yes, it will carry with it deep, low sounds of hurt, but also light, high notes of joy and refreshing. Your life will house both the highs and lows of a life given for Love. What is your anthem?

My promise was beginning to be reborn, slowly but surely. There were times when I thought I would never get back up. Instances—days, even months—where defeat seemed to eclipse any hope of life. When our dreams are reborn, power comes right along with them.

Remember Nicodemus in the Bible? There he was, Nick at night who couldn't wrap his head around the fact that he would be reborn. It was unthinkable. It went completely against natural law. It was even foolish. But it was truth. Ole Nick would have to unlearn all of his training and find simplicity in the beginning—a new beginning and rebirth.

And that new beginning is where I was awakened once more. In the newness I would be given authority beyond my weakness.

Learning to Receive

In the midst of this deep dark desert that I found myself in, many of my friends left. Only a few would stay by my side. They would give me a gift that would change my life. Though at times, they would have to wrestle me down to impart it! There will be times when we are rejected in the process. To everyone around us, we should just accept the death and move on, right? Even when it looks upside down, God asks us to trust when it goes against the crowd around us.

Did you notice that Mary's time of waiting extended over the Jewish Sabbath? Remember when I reminisced with you about Israel's fall of the Sabbath on Friday evening? One minute life was in full swing, and the next all was still, with no noise allowed to show itself. That is how it can seem in our own lives when our promise dies before us. Mary had to wait over the Sabbath—a time of consecrated rest. She would have to learn to rest in the middle of her turmoil, her questions, and her pain. How does that work?

Learning to rest is a hard lesson to grapple with. At least for me it was! My heart definitely was not at ease. But our seasons of waiting or weeping hinge on our ability to learn to rest in who we know God is. There are some things we can learn from information, but still others that we can only grasp by experiencing them for ourselves.

I was learning to join the margins as one of them. Only then could I receive what I truly needed. I had to switch seats—get out of my chair of giving, power, and answers—and sit low in the dust of need, expectancy, and openness. I had to face the fragility of my own existence.

We can learn from Mary's life. Those three days show us something about Heaven. When we carry and birth a promise into the earth, we give all of ourselves—we really do throw our lives away for its sake. Mary had given her entire life—everything she was. But God would give Mary something that was hard to receive—a time of hiddenness where He could be alone with her. It was almost as if time was transported back to the beginning, to that night where Heaven broke into her life unannounced. Her promise hinged on one thing—her relationship with the One who held life and death in His hands.

Mary had to learn to receive from Heaven. Sometimes when we are the ones who give of ourselves, we forget our position of lowliness. We shut out the fact that we need help, too! The truth is, we all need a time of hiddenness with God. No, this is not another formula to try to conjure up—it is a gift. Mary was empty, and her empty life needed to be filled up once more. What would come forth from her brokenness would shake the earth in a way that the first birthing of her promise could have never done alone.

Can You Find a Pulse?

Looking out the coffee shop window, I cupped my coffee in my hands, trying to adjust to the winter weather of the west that I had forgotten. I felt like a little child whose new toy had been broken beyond repair in front of her. My heart was broken, and I wondered where I would go from there. I tried creating my own life plans several times over without any avail.

Checking for a sign of life, I longed for one kick or movement that would remind me that everything was going to be OK. Feeling nothing, I decided to go work out at the gym nearby. With music in my ears, I began jogging on the treadmill with others around me. Working out is a way for me to connect with Jesus. I stuff some worship music in my ears and I begin mulling over memories of times when God just showed up. This day was no exception.

As I cranked up a fast-tempo song in my ears, I ran a little faster. As a blur caught my eye—a young guy beside me tripped on the treadmill and went into a seizure. Screams flooded the gym, and I yelled for someone to dial 911. Ripping the earphones out of my ears, I looked down at the guy whose body had now grown limp without a sign of life. He wasn't breathing. His mother knelt beside him, hysterically calling his name.

The young man began breathing again after a couple rounds of CPR. Disoriented, he began shaking, wrestling with those around who were help-ing. As the ambulance came and took him in stable condition to the hospi-tal nearby, I was beginning to realize just how much my own life mirrored his that day.

I, too, was holding on for dear life. There were no vital signs about my life that would lead me to thinking my promise would return. It was gone, there were no signs of life, and each day I was in panic mode. I needed spiritual CPR.

Don't let the signs fool you. When there is no pulse to be found, when you can't feel the heartbeat, the cadence that keeps your promise alive will come back. When vital signs are missing, CPR encompasses two avenues— breathing and compression. A force that only a touch can do.

There are times when we are empty in life and we simply need to be filled up. We need an external force to jump start our hearts back to work-ing as they have been created to do. When there is no way we can do it ourselves, we need others to help—to stand in the gap in the valleys of our lives and inject us with life.

God is on our side. He sends us spiritual EMS on the road when we cannot function on our own strength. When everything inside of us lies limp, He can bring life bustling with energy and growth. Do you need to be revived?

Can the Dead Be Reborn?

Looking out the window, I could see the clouds beneath me. Peering out of the small airplane window, a splash of sunshine was beginning to catch my hand. As I glanced down, a small rainbow landed on my palm. It was a sign of a living and breathing promise. It was a signal of new life and joy.

Just the week before—even the last year—had been a time of such stillness, deep hurt, questions, and confusion that were either met with offense or hiding. Yet this week had been different. The tide in my story was beginning to turn.

I came as a mess. Everyone knew it. There was no hiding anymore. No attempt at masking what was happening. I didn't really give a rip anyway. There was too much at stake. This was my life, not make-believe. So there I was, completely transparent in front of these people, and for the first time in my life it was safe.

Sometimes God gives us lifesavers along the way. People who love so profoundly that they are willing to dive to the depths of our darkness with us, sit with us in our mess, in our literal hells, and somehow grab hold of us and not let go until we both reach safety. Now *that's* love. It's messy. It hurts. It *really* hurts. But it never fails—*ever*.

Bob and Gracie[2] have been lifesavers in my life. I met Bob in Africa a couple of years before. When he taught, his ideas were so utterly foreign to me that the head-spinning they created irked me to pieces! Little did I know that those irkings would begin a conversation that has still continued to this very day.

I flew to Bob and Gracie's home near Seattle, Washington. I have never before met people like them who carry humility and power in such high levels. Their lives are filled with such miracles, and yet they have captured a side of Heaven on earth that very few get to witness firsthand. Their hearts have been the very things that have amazed me the most. The first week I was with them was filled with some of the most shocking presence of God that I have encountered in my small life. A year later I would return, completely upside down from where I had been.

They had both kept up with everything that was happening in my life. I can remember feeling so alone, and Bob would call most days and spend an hour reminding me of what God had promised me. His voice was the only constant that kept me from giving up. When I met them and their community, I was flabbergasted. I ran into a group of people who were OK with being a mess—OK with being broken. A place where being transparent about the horrors of our lives was normal and real. It spun my head even more! I had found a new home where there was freedom to be real and raw.

On my second trip out, both Bob and Gracie knew exactly where I was. We didn't need to tiptoe; we just jumped head-first into what I so desperately needed God to do. For four hours, they would pray over me, hold me, and sit with me while God ripped a shroud of death off my life.

Growing up I was taught a half-truth about forgiveness. Forgiveness to me was simply forgetting the offense and moving on with no questions asked. When Bob began talking about feeling through offenses done to us, there went my feeble mind again—dancing in all different directions of questions. I thought I understood forgiveness. Wow, was I wrong!

Acknowledging the offenses brought against me was the most intense time of my life. For once, I was not only able but asked to be honest with what I felt and about the consequences that had flowed into my life. I was given a gift to be completely open and vocal about what was happening. That was the only door that could yield true forgiveness.

Mary knew what violence felt like, sweeping her own life. Instinct tells me that you probably have as well. Acknowledging what has been done to us is the only way to fully forgive. Full forgiveness breaks us free from the captivity that we have known before. It cuts the strings that have tied us down and allows us to live in a manner of complete freedom.

The Holy Spirit comes down to rescue us when we are desperate for who He can only be. After praying that day, I came back into the Ekblad's home exhausted. My mind felt like Jell-O®, and my body felt like someone had hit me with a baseball bat a hundred times over. I couldn't even chew for lunch. All I wanted to do was close my eyes and be.

"How are you feeling?" Bob asked when I stumbled in. When I told him, he just chuckled. "That's usually how it is. Looked like a lot was happening there huh?" I nodded, unable to form any words.

A tide had been turned in my life—a page flipped over. I was on a path that would lead me straight toward another collision with the revival of my promise.

A Second Eclipse

I needed to be overshadowed again. What does that look like? I needed something to completely eclipse the blanket of despair that had covered my life for over a year. When our promise dies before us or within us, there is always a new birth that can take place.

"The Holy Spirit will come upon you, and the power of the Most High will overshadow you" (Luke 1:35 NIV). Some of us need to be overshadowed again. We need for Heaven to burst in unannounced and break once more into our chaotic lives. God wants you and me to see and witness—to carry His power in the realm around us.

When circumstances kill the life inside of us, Heaven has the final say. God wants to equip us with an upstaging from His heart. He wants to cause us to have courage to pay the price when everything is dead in us, when all things come against us. Will we count all of these things joy?

This new eclipse couples need with fullness—again a marriage of opposites. God is in the business of multiplication. He doesn't promise us a life free from pain and destruction. But He does vow to us all of His strength and power at our fingertips. He is pleased to give us everything He is and has. Do you need to be overshadowed again?

Endnotes

1. Dr. Heidi G. Baker, director, Iris Ministries, Inc., www.iris-min.org.

2. Dr. Bob and Gracie Ekblad direct Tierra Nueva and New Earth Refuge in Burlington, Washington, and Honduras, www.bobekblad.com.

Chapter 10

A Broken Life

"There is no one more beautiful than one who is broken!" —Watchman Nee

When we see and experience great beauty and great destruction, the hard questions come our way. Why are those who mourn blessed? How can that be a blessing? What about the poor and the hungry? How can starving and being barren be an honor? How can being beaten or attacked be a beautiful thing? That seems absurd, doesn't it?

…Everyone was trying to touch Him—so much energy surging from Him, so many people healed! Then He spoke:

> *You're blessed when you've lost it all. God's kingdom is there for the finding. You're blessed when you're ravenously hungry. Then you're ready for the Messianic meal. You're blessed when the*

tears flow freely. Joy comes with the morning. Count yourself blessed every time someone cuts you down or throws you out, every time someone smears or blackens your name to discredit Me. What it means is that the truth is too close for comfort and that that person is uncomfortable. You can be glad when that happens—skip like a lamb, if you like!—for even though they don't like it, I do...and all Heaven applauds. And know that you are in good company; My preachers and witnesses have always been treated like this (Luke 6:17-23).

Those who mourn, the poor, the hungry, the weary, the dying, and the abused all share a common ground. It is the simplicity of utter dependence and need. The door is wide open for Jesus to come in and assume His rightful name as Rescuer, Protector, Defender, and Redeemer. Their dependence, our helplessness, my need, and your weakness are irresistible to God.

We can learn from the poor what it really means to inherit the Kingdom of God. *"Blessed are the poor in spirit, for theirs is the Kingdom of Heaven"* (Matt. 5:3 NIV). Incarnational love is the choice to come into and love in the midst of a culture. If Jesus was our model, He has shown us what true incarnational love must look like. God left glory for the dirt. He humbled Himself and made Himself nothing. This, too, is for us.

Just as Jesus came into a new culture—the realm of humanity—and had to learn to walk and talk like the people He came to save, we are to do the same, emptying who we are and being possessed by the Spirit of God. This is a place where we recognize that, without Him, we can do nothing.

It is easy to view a life lived in love and its outworking from a idealistic perspective. Right as it is, it is only half of the truth of what the Gospel carries. I remember hearing that the cup that Jesus would offer us would be a cup of both suffering and joy. At one point, I had only known one end of that charge. The suffering, however, is a mysterious piece of His call that I have yet to even begin to grasp in my mind, but have little by little—and sometimes in large tangible ways—experienced firsthand. A broken life carries with it a magnetic attraction to Heaven. When we begin to awaken to our own fragility and need, we allow God to interject His fullness into our lives—a real-life spiritual BOTOX® is what I call it!

Living in the reality of a broken life frees us to cease from striving and yield to the process going on within our own hearts. Our stories carry with them power. Our greatest time of brokenness can become our most defining hour of preparation for what is to come in our futures.

On an Uneven Road

The small airport was crowded and bustling with noise and frustration. Randi and I had reconnected in France—me from Russia and Randi from Mozambique—and now we were stuck in a line that mirrored amusement park record lengths. Chaos was an understatement. Looking around, scowls on many faces let me know something was wrong. What could it be?

Our French had grown only a little in the four weeks we had spent in Paris and the countryside. We were left waiting in anticipation for the final verdict until an English speaker could be located.

At four in the morning, we had traveled an hour north of Paris to a small airport in the French "boonies," only to be told moments after arrival that our plane had been canceled. We were now stranded in the middle of nowhere in France! My continued sarcasm was an unwelcome addition to the morning hassles.

Looking around us, we sat down on the floor to reevaluate our options. What on earth were we going to do now? With the option of remaining in France or walking to Italy, we were exhausted. The next flight out of the country was not for another 24 hours. We hopped a bus back to Paris and decided to brainstorm on our way.

On the ground, we were left at a crossroads in the city. Glancing up, I saw a train station in front of us. It was worth a shot. We scuffled into the large terminal, and after waiting in line for what seemed like forever, we frantically grabbed some tickets and decided to trek into Italy in an unconventional way—a nearly 20-hour train ride crossing the French and Italian borders.

Holy Given

Stepping onto Rome's rustic streets, we marveled at the size of the building's structure. Cheeky actors dressed as ancient Roman soldiers lined the entranceway to the gigantic Coliseum. We placed our hands upon one of the inside walls and felt the rough stone that had been erected so long ago.

Within its interior rang the sounds of bloodshed like nowhere else known in history. Sitting down next to the holding cell, I noticed bars that led down to the underground chambers where those headed for death were held in their final moments. I could suddenly see a glimpse of what life would have looked like so long ago.

Flashes of sounds, screams, light, color, and tears flickered in front of me. Some 70,000 people would fill the large stadium, equipped with bloodthirsty jeers and pronouncements. To my right was a monument for the many who had died for their witness of God in the earth. Some were children so small. Others were women who were mothers, wives, daughters, and sisters. Men were those who left their families fatherless for the sake of an eternal mandate. Lions were unleashed on even the small, all for the sake of amusing a crowd—for entertainment and perverse pleasure. The martyr's battle cry was simple: "All this I do for love."

The cries of those who gave their lives for Jesus still echo through time. Down by my flip-flop, I noticed a small stalk of wheat growing up from the ground of the prison gate. Their sacrifice had not been in vain, but yielded fruit way beyond their time.

What does it mean to throw your life away? To count it as nothing in comparison to our spirit's cry? The Moravians carried this same heartbeat— the rhythm that we have been conversing about this entire time. It is a battle cry that trades violence for love—the same love that gives itself for its enemy. It becomes a life that turns bloodshed on its head and embraces enemy-love—a people, a new tribe that has chosen to carry an anthem of abandon. Their song is their story—"Worthy is the Lamb who was slain"—as they follow in His footsteps. Our perspectives on a life lived in love are changing and being overturned. We have been invited to catch a fresh look at what it means to give your entire life in exchange for a Kingdom that does not end.

A Fresh Look

A new, fresh look at suffering and joy gives us an angle of the power of a broken life. It is our weakness married to God's power that can shake the earth at its very core. Embracing it is the hard part because it goes against all we have ever been taught as truth. It defies our cultural norms and expectations.

Only those who have been trained in the wilderness can be true keepers of God's heart. Only people who have been broken beyond repair can bring unmistakable healing and freedom. Those who know hiddenness with God get to make their home in His presence. When you can truly dwell with the poor and the unlovely, Heaven can trust you with all of its riches and resources. "Those who suffer at the hands of a sin-sick world can take captivity captive. To become the friends of God we must learn obedience as humble servants."[1]

The definition of revival is transforming. We have got to be honest and real on a gut level. Being real together about our spiritual need is where we all begin. This bottoms-up Kingdom is just that. It starts from a shared place of desperation.

You are a candidate for a radical visitation from God when you are a "nobody," a failure, even a mess. Keep pressing through. Some of you are so discouraged that you have stopped right before your season would change. Jesus is attracted to honest lives. We all need help!

Do you want to be a partner in a coming move of God in the earth around you? Do you desire to bridge Heaven? Historic renewal movements—revivals of the past—have not lasted. Why is that? While we know that seasons change, a global move of the Holy Spirit will only last when we unite in transparent worship. We exhaust ourselves to make the cut in life and appease our retirement plans, our families, and other external expectations that keep us on a constant hamster wheel of activity and endless self-advancement.

We were meant to let Heaven burst through the earth, but we were not meant to decide where the wind would blow. We must be willing to become people of the tent who follow the movement that God is playing in our world. A "movement" of God is just that. It is forever moving, changing, forming, and growing. In order to continue on it, we must be willing to be flexible, too.

Through the Back Door

"The low place"[2] is an intentional posture we are invited to lunge into. Coming from a Western perspective, mission work—a lifestyle of following Jesus—was always carried out on our terms. The "us" and "them" mentality was in full reign. We were forever seated in a chair of dominance, even if our motives were good. I can remember as a teenager serving at a Christmas outreach service that gave canned foods and coats to the needy. The look in the woman's eyes standing opposite me as she took the coat and canned goods from my hands said what no one had ever had the courage to tell me in plain words. Even my "charity" was on my terms. I had no idea what it was like being a mother with children to provide for in the inner city, as the woman staring into my eyes knew. Yet somehow, I was on the paramount end while she was the one forced to expose her lack and need. Somewhere deep within me, I knew I was just like that lady somehow. That day, I was just given the option to mask it, as the one "giving" and the one with a full stomach.

We can learn a lot from the way life has been walked out by the Christian Church in history. We have committed a lot of costly mistakes. Much of the third world has seen the devastating effects of lives given for a love synchronized with other agendas and other allegiances that tainted its outworking, from colonialism to imperialism and modern-day globalization and war.

In Africa, the West brought a picture of Jesus covered in a polished suit and tie. What happened in the aftermath was that revival looked like people wearing suits and ties that mirrored the distorted picture of God they were so overly gorged with.

What Jesus are we bringing to the world? A large lesson we have to learn—hopefully sooner rather than later—is that we cannot assume the place of dominance when we go out into the world to bridge Heaven and earth. Working with the rich, the poor, the old, or the young means that we sit with them in their lives and feel what they feel. In that place is a joining where we can together bring God's presence into our normal lives, no one above or below the next.

Beauty for Ashes

God hears our cries, our groans. When we are in captivity, Heaven's eyes are still on us. There are times when we feel our voice is not being heard. Everyone has a voice. There are no voiceless ones in the Kingdom of God. He hears all of us in our pits of need, and those outcries grab hold of His heart.

When our promises are dead, we need to be candidly honest about our wounds. Otherwise, we're going to have shallow revival. In order for real, heavy, full renewal to come, we have to allow the depths of our hearts to have a voice. When God visits us, He isn't going to just visit the religious elite. He visits the lowly, the unthinkable, the failures.

Our cries are met with His words of who we are. We have to lose our life to find it—give up our dream to receive it back. Let go of control to find true freedom. The Kingdom seems to get more upside down than ever just before our dreams are brought back to life.

The Rebirth of a Dream

The promise was reborn. No one remembered or understood that this would take place. No one knew He would come back. Mary saw where He was laid. There was another shaking as the angel revisited. The stone was rolled away. Heaven again broke in unannounced. When the time of rest was over, new life came charging in.

Jesus was alive. Holy chaos rushed in again! New life and new power was with them. He had gone and taken the keys to Heaven and hell. Now, Heaven was bursting in victorious. When we give our promise up, we allow an opportunity to receive it back in greater measure than when we began. Mary was learning this very lesson that first Easter morning.

Lose your life and you will find it. Coming out the other end—the backside or back door of mourning—leads us to joy. Mary was given new eyes to see in the midst of her suffering and the suffering of Jesus. Heaven gave her joy that was her strength. She had just given up her hope and let go of control. Only after she let go of her promise was it given back to her in fullness, in maturity, and in power.

When Mary's promise was first whispered to her, it was not tangible. When it was birthed into the earth, it was immature, unripe, and weak. It would have to grow, develop, and be patient only to die. The death of her promise yielded power beyond all she could have ever imagined.

When the promise came back to life, it came in fullness, depth, intensity, and wholeness. Only through the demise of her destiny was she able to experience her promise in power. Mary's promise was now reborn. The old was now gone, and the newness astounded everyone, including herself!

Who Will Roll the Stone?

Mary could not revive her promise. The morning air was crisp as she flung open the door of her home, exposing herself to the world around her for the first time in the last three days. "It is time to let go," she thought.

Running to the gravesite, Mary clutched a small bottle of spices and oil. She was ready to give everything that was dead inside of her to Heaven and leave it at His feet. Tears ran down her cheeks as she got nearer to the tomb.

Mary was aware of her weakness in a deeper way than ever before. Looking up at the large stone that stood between her and her dream, she realized she couldn't roll the stone away. She wasn't strong enough and she needed help. But who would come to her rescue?

As she looked again, a familiar light stood before her. The same illumination that she encountered in the beginning was in front of her. The stone was rolled back, and the doorway was open for her to enter in. She wondered, "What is all of this for?"

Looking inside, the remains of her promise were gone, with nothing but a few rags that had covered her son. "Has someone taken Him?" she questioned frantically.

Seeing her fear, the angel interrupted in his usual nature. "Mary, don't cry. Your promise is alive. He is not dead, but has come back to life. Don't you understand? He did this for you and for those around you. Death could not keep Him away from you. He has battled death and won!"

Mary was blindsided by this news. What was happening? She had been ready to give up her dream, and now another fork in the road that no one on earth could have prepared her for was in front of her. "Where is He?" she asked within herself.

In her silence, the angel heard her. "Leave no one out. For what you have given will not be forgotten. The world will be changed from this day on. Go, run, and you will see Him soon!"

Without a word, Mary ran, just as the day she met up with Elizabeth so long before. Her time of waiting soon turned into a time of urgency. Her spirit leaped from within her again. Her promise had been reborn!

What brought it back to life? Heaven did. God rolled the stone away on the tomb of Mary's promise. We can feel stuck in this season of weeping. We can feel forever captive. I did. Only God can roll away the stone. He is the only one who can reawaken, bring forth, and enliven our hope—what He had placed inside of us—and call it out once more.

Magic Wand Faith

My life has been as much a wrestling match with God as it has been a journey. Sometimes the answers to the hard questions in life have to be hit head-on, and that collision can take awhile to recover from! I knew, from the moment that I took my first step into deciding to learn in an upside-down way in the world, that giving up my possessions would be the easiest of tasks. The real challenge was in relinquishing control of the ways that I had always walked out my life.

In asking the hard questions, I wondered how such disaster could engulf the world around me, and yet there would be pockets or sometimes waves of places where God would show up and "magically" make things "better." Was the life of following Jesus a "hit and miss" game of chance where we would cross our fingers and hope that Heaven would flip a coin and land in our favor?

How does an upside-down, inside-out Kingdom function? The Kingdom of Heaven is continuously a merger of the most paradoxical thoughts. It is here and not yet. How can those two realities coexist together? Why does healing come to some and not others? Why does disease plague parts of the world and health reign in others? Why are some full and others starving? What's more, how can both house God's presence?

God loves our questions. Working through these seasons and not dismissing them can bring us freedom like never before. This wrestling is what draws us close to Jesus more than ever. In that place is where we can come nearer to Him, face to face, where restraint and hesitation are not welcome. I am still contending through questions I have in life. What I do know is that the answers can only come from Him. When I shy away and look for them in other places, I am left void or more confused at best. The Bible makes it clear that, *"Love and truth meet in the street..."* (Ps. 85:10). This is an invitation into a tag-team match of asking the hard questions in life. When we encounter God in everyday life, in the streets and alleyways of our ordinary existence, we can see reality for what it really is.

The Undercover Exchange

There is a divine switch that happens when we are honest about our hurts, our questions, our joys, and our longings. When we give God all that we are—including the ugly, the suffering, and the painful parts—He trades us. In our empty hands, void of any of our own strength, He places power and His presence, which turns everything around. Reflecting on this upside-down Kingdom can send us on a journey to find more. It stirs our hunger to keep trekking until we find the homeland that we have been created for.

We are living too much in concepts today. No amount of teaching can grow us if it is not experiential. Information is great. But without tangible action, it is merely theory in our lives. We need to begin to live out of a place of experience—a place of encounter. Who is the Jesus that you know? Does He mirror encounters that others have had and told you about? Or is He real enough that you have met with Him yourself? Is your faith based more on concepts or experiential reality?

There are times when seasons of waiting give way to times of urgency. The times of resting—even Mary's three days—had an ending. They didn't last forever. The movement she found herself within was constantly moving. Our lives are no different. Some of us wait so long to move on to our destinies. I have heard people tell me hundreds of times over that they were "waiting for a sign" of what to do. Yet within their hearts, they burned for a promise that they knew was for them. They knew what their dream was—they knew what it looked like. They were just looking for permission to go. But the permission was already there, waiting for them to initiate their promise.

Sometimes God asks us, "What do you want to do?" That longing in our hearts—the heartbeat that we carry—is living and growing inside of us and cannot remain in there, sheltered and covered up forever. It must be birthed and come out and mature in the world around us.

Are you willing to respond to the rhythm inside of you? Can you feel it moving and pulsating within your spirit? Do you know what God has promised you? You may feel like it is dead. Yet even in the defeat, are you willing to step out and trust?

Finding Our Homeland

We are all on a path that is sometimes so curvy that we can dizzy ourselves along the ride. In the beginning of this heart-to-heart discussion, I mentioned the wandering that we are all invited on. Its end result is finding our home in God.

Home is our ultimate quest. A spiritual homeland for us will mean much more than a place to rest. It will encompass all that we are and aim for. Our lives are a constant journey—a nomadic trek that leads us to the place we were made for. When we are cast out, we run to Him.

Every living thing contains a need to belong—to be known and to be wanted. We long to love and be loved. Without both, there is something inside of us left unfulfilled and unsatisfied. Without Heavenly interference, Mary might have been content going through life as usual. She might not have been asking for it, expecting it, or hoping for it, but she was hand-picked for the miraculous.

Ask yourself now—where are you headed? What is the destination your life aims for? For my own life, there has been a constant and sometimes snail-like transition from feeling as if I needed to "tiptoe" in God's house to recognizing that I could run through loudly in a place that I belonged and even had my inheritance and ownership in. There was a "click" in my heart and my mind that took place when I realized that I was no longer a guest but a part of the family in God's Kingdom. Everything inside of His house was given to me. All the rooms, all the nooks and crannies were shared with me because I carried His name and His imprinting.

The upheavals of our theological mind-sets that do not line up with God's heart are defining moments in our lives. Our "God in a box" theories are constantly disintegrating when Heaven invades our lives. When we understand that bridging Heaven and earth is something innately given to us as sons and daughters in God's Kingdom, our focus changes from seeking secret (and may I add expensive) formulas to realizing we have been paying for something we had at our fingertips all along—free of charge.

Endnotes

1. Graham Cooke, author and speaker, www.grahamcooke.com.

2. Dr. Heidi G. Baker, director, Iris Ministries, Inc., www.iris-min.org.

Chapter 11

Laid-Down Love

He must increase, but I must decrease (John 3:30 NKJV).

One of the most sideways gifts I have ever unwrapped was unlearning some of my formal theological training. The "God in a box" package is manufactured, shipped, and sold throughout cultures around the world. It does have a price tag many times and is often protected against tampering or outside interference. Sometimes, it just doesn't fit within life in the real world.

Relearning the ways of a child is a priceless enlightenment. Tradition, good or bad, is often protected, preserved, and passed down. There will always be a cost in asking questions. Thankfully, the price tag is mild compared to the freedom it will yield.

Laid-down love carries a similar fee. Let's unpack this lifestyle a bit. Just what is a life laid down for love? What does it look like in our everyday lives? We give ourselves away—all that we are, all that we want to be—at Jesus' feet. We leave it for Him and follow after where He goes.

God wants to love us to death. It is shocking, I know. That is His nature! His personality means that He sees the end result and sticks with us through the good, the bad, and the ugly of our lives in order to get there. He sees farther than we do and cheers us on to cross the finish line to the unveiling of our destinies. He relishes in our small, short lives. He finds such beauty and curiosity that draws Him to participate with us in our journey.

We have been created to burn with something that transcends ourselves. What do you burn for? What makes you tick? When you wake up in the morning, what are you thinking about? There are times in our lives where we must begin to push aside all of the "have-tos" in life and embrace the "what-ifs." What have you been made for?

When the dream is reborn, we have a chance to run again. It is a chance to recommit to our promise. An opportunity to reinvest in what is inside of us—what has been called out in us from the very beginning.

Surrender is a hard process. To abandon our lives for something beyond ourselves, something that goes farther than we ever will, something much bigger than our few breaths and years. This is our chance to be a part of a movement that does not end but that is breathing, living, and forever moving around us.

Reawakened to an inner longing, I began to feel the heartbeat of Heaven within my own life. I'm still learning how to quiet myself when chaos storms around me, just to hear that sometimes-faint rhythm. But it does remain!

This Kingdom is trusted to the childlike. My greatest teachers have all been under the age of five. Instead of growing up, we grow down. It's so completely paradoxical that our instinct to make something of ourselves is offended and hopefully obliterated along the way.

When the Dust Settles

The melody of drumming filled the hot Sudanese night. As usual, it was so steamy that even the mosquitoes had fled the scene. Stumbling out of my room, children—some 50 of them—were clapping, dancing, and singing at the top of their little lungs in radiant joy. Little boys grabbed empty jerry cans that we used for water and began beating on them as makeshift drums. The cadence flowed into the air around us like a streaming river in the deep blue night.

Looking down to my right, I joined Talia and others, hopping on one foot and then the other. Awkwardly, I attempted to mimic their immaculate twirls and leaps. Their patience waited for me in giggles that said it all.

I watched the little toddler next to me whip around in her little dress and bare feet, creating a whirlwind or tornado of dust in the wake of her presence. Little coos and shrieks soon accompanied the song that now enveloped the tiny dirt courtyard.

The children had caught something so foreign to what I had ever known in my own life. They had found that emptiness was a gateway to fullness. It was, in fact, a wide-open door to enter in before them. They would not be left in their need, but would be met with an all-encompassing answer that would overwhelm and overfill their little lives whenever they needed.

Need and hunger were gifts in their eyes. They had known hunger, sadness, pain, loss, and exposure. They had been given all of that turned on its head—fullness, joy, and shelter—family in all its messiness and beauty. Each of these found within one glance.

They had found a home and shown me the way to go to find it for myself. They invited me into their world—a place of wonder, which I still find so incredibly difficult to describe. The way in was small, low, and really at times quite awkward!

In the heat of the darkness that night, with sweat beading down my cheeks as I shimmied hand in hand with the littlest of these, I had to get on my knees to spin around in their game of worship and dance. As the dust and ground brand-ed my knees, I found an answer to a question I didn't even know I had to ask.

I was beginning to see that no matter what the cost, saying "yes" to God's promise over our lives would all be worth it in the end. When every-thing is said and done, what will matter? What will be remembered when the dust settles? Tangible love will redefine our lives. In order for you and I to see Heaven on earth—the unveiling and flourishing of what is inside of us, our destinies in the world around us—we have to be willing to first and continuously allow and invite Heaven to invade our little lives. We can only give what we have received.

Side by side with two- and three-year-olds, I met with Jesus. I was catch-ing another glimpse of a gift along the way—the realization that it would not all be cost. And just as opposites marry one another in this Kingdom I had stepped into, cost would soon flip into reward.

Carrying to Full Term

What is it about God that He would choose to use a little laid-down girl in the dirt when He handpicked Mary? Why does He want to use you? You don't know? It is because you are loved. God looks at you and says, "I can pos-sess them and make my home in their lives. I can give them the joy of carrying the promise to full-term. I can journey with them each step of the way."[1]

God has given you a promise. There will be times when you can feel the kicks of the life within you. There will also be times when everything seems still and life seems to cease. The promise seems distant and disconnected. There are many lives throughout time, including today, that have prematurely flushed out the life and dreams inside of them. But Heaven wants to see the unveiling and the maturing of the gifts inside of us—for our destinies to be fulfilled and nothing, no part of them, to be left unturned or undone.

The sad thing about ministry is that there are so many abortions in the spiritual realm. He is calling people to carry the promise that

He has placed within them to full term. That means that there will be a cost. It means there will be a reproach. It means not everyone will understand.[2]

I am sure Mary received a great reproach both before her promise was birthed and after her promise had died. Think about what her closest allies—family even—would have told her. The typical "I told you so" speech would not cut it. The entire destiny of humanity hinged on her promise, on her "yes," and on her persevering when times got tough. It meant pressing on when times seemed out of control and chaotic. It meant believing when others, even confidants, said otherwise. God sets before us life and death. He lets us choose which one we will side with.

Spiritual abortions threaten all of us at one time or another in our lives. Inwardly, there is always a choice for us to say "no" or "It's too much; I have to stop." Confusion and doubt can become instruments of extraction that can take what is inside of us and rip it to shreds. Externally, voices from others—directly or indirectly—can cause waves of hurt and misunderstanding and times when accusations will trick us into believing them as truth. There will be times when there are simply no words to communicate what Heaven has placed inside of you and is going to do in the world through you.

The enemy of true life has always been about aborting life inside of us. From the beginning until now, he knows that a life lived in fullness is a great danger and threat to what he has established in the earth. But your promise will shake and dismantle generations of sin in the world around you. There is power inside of you. We have been asked to carry the promise to full term. That means through the birthing and then through the death, to the other side of life and the rebirth—the resurrection of a God-breathed dream.

Empty Lives

The sounds of giggles outside of my "window"—a small open slat screen held up by a few iron bars—were my waking alarm clock. I opened my eyes and realized that I had a large smile on my face. Maybe it was expectancy of what this special day would entail? Maybe I just had a good dream? I wasn't sure. One thing I knew, I was running late!

I stumbled outside of the same small room in Mozambique held up by the same feeble dirt wall where my story all began. I wrapped my *katanga* around my waist and quickly threw on some waterproof mascara and a pair of flip-flops, rushing outside into the humid African "wild." Today would be a distinct day for everyone who would gather.

Hundreds of people from all walks of life, from countries around the world, found themselves side by side with African pastors and friends underneath the infamous tent. The sunshine flooded under the large green-and-white-striped tent that we had all come to know as a second home. The drums and, yes, the ancient keyboard that we rigged up resonated through the crowd and out into the village around us. A new rhythm yet a familiar beat was flowing through each of us with force that morning. As the cadence rang through the atmosphere, we were all beginning to catch the beat as our bodies imitated its nature.

Dancing lasted for hours. There were no fans, no air conditioning, just the soaring body heat that engulfed the air around us creating a virtual sauna in our midst. Why were we dancing? We were finally realizing that we were free and that it was actually possible to live a life of being possessed by God.

As evening hit, we were still dancing. Let's just say Richard Simmons had nothing on us! We were dancing like we were in a never-ending marathon of twirls and jumps. As the sun began to sink in the horizon, a great cotton-candy-colored sky swirled around us. The rhythm of the ocean's waves beating down in the final push of the day's tide complimented the pulsating worship we were caught in.

With that, we called up to the front all of those who had taken three months out of their lives to meet with God. These students had come from places all over the world—the north, the south, the east, and the west. This night was their "graduation"—a launching that would send many of them out, not back "home," but into other corners of the earth that they hadn't expected upon arrival.

They came empty. During their time immersed in living, loving, and learning among the poorest of the poor, they had caught gifts of hunger and dependence on Heaven alone. They had met with God in a way that they couldn't have done anywhere else. They had accessed the heart of Jesus and grabbed onto it with all of their might. Now, in that moment, it was time to be sent out and to give away what they had received with the same abandon that they arrived with.

As we had the African pastors pray over the students, Heaven broke loose. Students lay on the ground, scattered around in the dirt. They were being sent out from His face.

Empty lives were being filled with Heaven's fullness. This was bigger than who we were. It was not an isolated event where Jesus randomly decided to come and meet with us. This was a promise given to all of us that we were, together, reaching up and pulling down to our level.

We were getting invited deeper into the back door of a life given for Love. It would look different for all of us. There would be some who would, as Randi and I had a couple years before, don a backpack and skip off into the third world, carrying a light that could not be extinguished. Others would return to the West and sound an alarm to wake up those who had fallen into a deep sleep. Some would bring Heaven into banks and businesses. There would be some who would even set out to see the Kingdom of God erected in Hollywood and media outlets. Still others would carry completely unique and unheard-of visions into the deepest parts of the jungles of South America. We were being sent everywhere, and each of us carried a rare embodiment of this promise.

When Heaven Dances

The early morning sunshine cascaded down through the Judean hillside. Life had turned out to be completely outside of the box Mary had imagined and dreamt up. Walking to meet with the Way, she paused to tilt her head toward the fresh and sizzling beams of light from above. Taking a deep breath, Mary smiled, realizing everything had turned out OK. The angel was right. Heaven had kept its promise to her.

Her lifelong dream would remain with her for only 40 short days. The promise in her was finally matured—fulfilled right next to her. With it would come a new promise of signs and wonders following in the city and world. A promise of power would drop in Mary's lap as she watched the ascension of what she had given her life for.

Her promise would go out into all the earth. It would not end with her. It would sweep the globe for all remaining days. Mary's "yes" would echo in time through generations and would continue even when she would end. In those moments of pondering, she realized the words given her in the beginning—in her simple ordinary setting—were being confirmed.

Everyone had gathered with her that morning. Jesus with His last words shouted, "Receive!" Breathing on them, now each of them carried Heaven's scent. Their hearts were burning within them. As He unraveled the words she had been given they were left with two final gifts—His breath and His peace.

Mary watched the fulfillment of her dream as it ascended into Heaven. All that she had been promised was happening before her eyes, but in a way that she would have never expected. It was much better than she could work up on her own.

As Jesus rose through the clouds, a flashback in time flooded her eyes. The angel had said all she had to do was say "yes." Heaven would do the rest. Mary had learned to let go and given her promise back. Now her King was on His throne.

Heaven had danced with earth because she had persevered and believed. Yes, Jesus had done it. But Mary emptied herself out in giving her life away to Him. Suddenly, all those years hit her all in one glance. It was never about her anyway. This promise would transcend her for all of time.

The rebirth of Mary's promise rang into the earth for centuries to come. That is what true revival is! It is resurrection—a holy renaissance for us to experience together. In death, in our weakness, in our emptiness, Heaven can explode our lives with power that reveals His true nature. It is His reflection in our stare.

Paul, when writing about those before him who carried the promise, said:

> *Through acts of faith, they toppled kingdoms, made justice work, took the promises for themselves. They were protected from lions, fires, and sword thrusts, turned disadvantage to advantage... There were those who, under torture, refused to give in and go free, preferring something better: resurrection. Others braved abuse and whips, and, yes, chains and dungeons. We have stories of those who were stoned, sawed in two, murdered in cold blood; stories of vagrants wandering the earth in animal skins, homeless, friendless, powerless—the world didn't deserve them!—making their way as best they could on the cruel edges of the world* (Hebrews 11:32).

In the midst of our individual journeys in life, we look to those who have gone before us—those who carried the promise long ago. They chose more than temporary freedom. They picked the side of resurrection, knowing that in order for new life to come it must first be lifeless before them. A road of suffering is a chosen path that leads us to new life—renewal. And just as Paul wrote about what happened on the "edges" of the world, so we find the same powerful Jesus in the margins—the edges of our society—today.

His Presence Alone

We will live to see every color and every language joined together in a great rebirth. It is up to us to be doors for others to peer in, to step into this upside-down Kingdom. Programs will not change our world. Organizations, outreaches, and our own doings will not help people come alive to their core. It is His presence that makes us different. God has set up a camp on the margins—on the outskirts of our developments and attempts at becoming our own answer in the earth.

Will you follow Him to the least of these? And will you not just be there, but make your home in that location? It is one thing to help those on the margins and another completely to join them as one and the same. It means stepping down from our positions, just as Jesus did, and realizing the enormity of our own need. The overwhelming awareness that our voices of hunger together can create a roar that cannot be ignored.

God will give us encounters of promise even throughout the times when our dreams have died. He longs for us to see Him again for who He is in us! During my year of pause, in the midst of emptiness, I was given gifts—reminders that life would return in fullness. I began having dreams unleashed in the night that shook me to awaken to who I was and would become.

He is positioning us in a place of encounter. Mary's story mirrors ours. God interrupts our normal, everyday lives and turns everything on its head. Before us lies an invitation to take His hand again, to step into His big shoes one step at a time, and to follow.

The childlike are given the Kingdom. We are welcomed and helped to learn from children and to grow down instead of grow up. We can catch trust and abandon—the hallmarks of our homeland that are not beyond our reach.

Neema's Cries

Dripping wet from head to toe, I looked down at my ankle, bleeding to the ground with a flowing stream. We had just gotten back from baptizing a large group of people in the Indian Ocean across from where we called home. Now limping, soaking wet from head to toe, and injured from my leg getting caught on a rock, I walked back with a cluster of children hopping along with me.

As I drew closer to home, a friend of mine caught my attention with a wide-angled wave. "*Njo!* (Come here!)" he shouted in Kiswahili, asking me to come. I could hear the cries of his family's new baby cooing through their thatched walls. I had met his family more than a year before. Though we were in Mozambique and the primary language was Portuguese, he and his wife had once lived in Tanzania and knew I loved the Swahili language. Each day as we would spend time together as a family, I would talk in Swahili and he would translate into Portuguese. They would teach me mounds of words, and we sat on the ground with nothing but a worn-out pencil and recycled piece of crumpled paper.

I remember hearing cries coming from their small, one-room home as I inched nearer that day. It was a girl! Eight days old and full of bouncing and cooing life. Her parents looked at me and asked, "Would you name our baby? What is her name?"

I was shocked and in awe of the gift they would allow me to receive as part of the welcomed-in family. Mama handed the naked baby into my arms. Gazing down into those wide, dark blue eyes, I was taken back to a place years before in a country north of Mozambique.

In that encounter I was holding another little baby, though instead of eight days old, Neema was nine months of age. Born into the world with HIV, Neema had known suffering and joy all before the age of one in the earth. The day before she died, I held her, looking down into her eyes. Her reflection was masked with wisdom and peace, which I had no idea how to capture in my own life.

Now, years later, as I looked at the new baby girl in my arms, I was confronted with Neema in her eyes. My answer was found again in one stare. Her name would be Neema—"Grace" in Kiswahili. She would carry favor and blessing in the harsh world around her.

Life was coming full-circle for me. Perhaps I was catching a new glimpse of the companionship of opposites in the Kingdom of Heaven. Suffering would always give way to joy. Neema would carry enough love in the community around her to tip the scales to victory.

The Long Haul

When the storm rages in our lives, we are given a chance to hold on. Sticking in through the thick and thin parts of life is our choice. Some people choose to walk away in the middle of their songs. It can get hard—more difficult than human capability can handle. Lingering and remaining when we feel like running away—listening for the sign of life when we are told there is nothing left—this is for us.

It will be a long and sometimes rough road ahead of us. In theory there is no problem. But when we are hit face-first in our own lives, these ramblings take on an entirely different view. We were not meant to go alone. We need to team up for the path ahead.

Community is our key to keeping on the way in front of us. Others keep us going when we don't have the strength to continue on our own. We were meant to be a team who together trudge on in the trenches of life around us.

Stand on Your Head

You are positioning yourself for entry into this upside-down Kingdom by simply standing on your head. What does that look like? Allowing room for ourselves to feel out our boxes of belief will eventually throw us on our heads anyway. It's a good thing to open up our thinking to the breath of God. That does mean that there will be times when our ways of thinking will be challenged and sometimes obliterated!

It's not enough to just sit back and insulate our ideologies. We have to pursue God's presence. Are we willing to go anywhere to find it?

We have been given a divine curiosity for the presence and nature of God. Who is the God behind our encounters? These meetings and visitations are meant to catch our attention and lure us into searching after His nature and where He dwells. They are not merely an end to themselves, but reflect the light of His face—who He is.

We cannot do it without His presence. You cannot live a life and steer your promise alone. God waits for us in the pause to see where our curiosity lies. Will we jump in, even when the door seems camouflaged?

You can see the blind receive sight and the dead raised, but without knowing Jesus face to face it does not matter. After the angel leaves, where are you? What makes your heart burn within you when the illuminated encounter fades away?

The presence of God distinguishes us from the rest of the world. We are set apart when His face hovers over ours. It's the very thing that spins the heads of those who see nobodies like us who couldn't possibly make it through life on our own. A lifelong pursuit of the face of Jesus is our shared journey.

Heaven's Kiss

Many of us have felt the sting of seeing our promise die. Can you feel the beat begin again? We were created to echo Heaven's heartbeat. Can you hear the rhythm? Can you hear the sound of a dream reshaping? A promise made before time that could only come from outside of ourselves.

We have been born to know Heaven's kiss—the interaction that takes place when we open up who we are to all God is. Heaven's kiss is what can happen when we turn over our agendas, our fears, our reservations, and our hopes to join into what God is doing in the earth around us.

Your obedience opens the way for tens, hundreds, thousands, or possibly millions. You go where there is no path and blaze one for many to come.

The very epicenter of the supernatural is a place of laid-down love—the location where we toss aside everything and exchange all that we possess to gain an inheritance too heavy to carry alone. A kiss from Heaven imprints on us our spiritual DNA—an imprinting that cannot be washed away.

You were meant to experience the reality of God's hand for yourself. It is a promise that has been given to you before you were even thought of. In that kiss is healing, restoration, empowerment, and strengthening. It is a transaction that deposits in us who we have been created to become. This is your destiny—a life given for Love.

Endnotes

1. Dr. Heidi G. Baker, director, Iris Ministries, Inc., www.iris-min.org.

2. Ibid.

Chapter 12

A Gift of Hunger

Blessed are those who hunger and thirst for righteousness, for they will be filled (Matthew 5:6 NIV).

Another trip across the continent of Africa was underway. The early morning rays of sun were beaming down on my face like an alarm clock that morning. I rubbed the sleep from my eyes and was thrown up to the top of the bus as it collided with its millionth crater in the road—which was really a hole-covered dirt path—in front of us. Looking outside of my window, I was reawakened to an entire world I had forgotten about.

Thick fog billowed up from the Kenyan hills and mountainsides. Even though the bus was traveling at speeds unheard-of, there were moments when snapshots of the countryside seemed to stand still. Looking down at my journal, my "chicken scratch" scribbles struggled to be legible in the heart of a completely bumpy ride.

Amidst the hullabaloo around me, I started thinking of the path I had been on thus far in my life. I saw the children from countries around the world I had danced with. Flashes of spinning around with them caught my attention for what seemed like forever. Another realization came. The poor had given me a gift that no one else on earth could. Looking down through the memories, I discovered that I had now been in more countries than years I had been on the earth. How did I get to this place?

As I focused on the memories of the dances I had shared, I began to catch a view from an angle that I had never been at before. It was the poor teaching the rich how to eat from Heaven. A view of what the underside could transform into if we chose to stay there long enough for God to show up. A picture of the margins illuminated with Heaven's touch. This was the fingerprint that was smudging itself into our lives—my life. A spiritual tattooing that would never fade away.

This upside-down Kingdom boggles our minds. The ideas and methodologies that have been passed down to us sometimes don't measure up to Heaven's eye. We can do nothing apart from Him. Most of us come from a place where hunger is a nondefinitive word. In our experience, it carries with it little relevance and tangibility.

Heaven wants to freely give us gifts of hunger. We cannot muster it up on our own or achieve it through a checklist of requirements. We may not have it from where we have grown up or been raised, but we can receive it free of charge.

Life no longer means that we have to strive to become something we already are. Our journey gets redefined and looks little like we originally conceived in our tiny imaginations. That is precisely what God is longing for in our hour. It is the complete upheaval of our feeble imaginations—a reawakening to the prophetic imagination that calls out its promises in creation around us. It is the tangible presence of God that will set us apart from the rest of the earth. It will not be our accomplishments, our buildings, our money, or our credentials. Life suddenly takes on a different angle when we realize that that which we labored for so long was, in fact, free and in front of our noses the entire time!

Captivated by Heaven's Gaze

In the silence, He watches. The world moves in daily chaos. Wars, poverty, famine, and death abound. There are the hungry, the thirsty, the dying. Yet in the midst of such destruction, one thing remains. Love makes Himself known among us. Only this time Love is a person—a tangible reality. It is this Love we look to for peace and light.

In the stillness of Heaven's spotlight, do we know His eyes are upon us? Do we recognize Him behind such guises? Will we choose to see? The image-bearers of the Father captivate Heaven—and so is all of creation! In the silence, we find that we are part of something much larger than ourselves—a borderless Bride that has no end.

God's original longing was that His house would be full. What is the purpose of your life, you wonder? Bring in His kids. That is what we were meant to dance within. It is a journey to build a new family in front of our very eyes.

In the midst of war and the death of our promises within and around us, God can erect castles in the mud pits of our lives. Most of us struggle with the coexistence of the opposites of death and life, suffering and joy. There is a constant tension between the idea of the "haves" and the "have-nots." The earth was never meant to become this way. We do know that sometimes those who have nothing possess more than our large buildings could ever contain. Their small, open-air gatherings carry a presence of Heaven that could not be embraced by our familiar yet shallow four walls.

Drink Deeply

The scorching sand beneath my feet was a tad beyond bearable that afternoon. The hot tropical sun had already baked the earth below, and I was no exception! After teaching at the village school that morning, Khadija, a small but brave little girl, walked with me hand in hand to the little shack we depended on for cold, clean water. She was one of my "children posse" that forever stayed by my side. I can still see us dancing for hours on end as the girls laughed at my awkward stiffness. I would get better though… eventually!

Magugu village was one of the liveliest whistle stops I have ever landed in. The market was set up with colors encompassing the rainbow of veggies and fruits. Eyeing a delicious coconut, Khadija said it without words. And within seconds we were off, only this time with a coconut in our arms for dinner later that evening.

The mosque's prayers were extra loud that day. In a village of so very few, you'd think they could turn the volume down a little. No such luck. Let's just say I was never in need of an alarm clock while living there!

With a cold, fresh bottle of water in each of our hands, we started back, almost jogging from the sand's blazing heat below us. As we neared the mosque, I noticed an old man sitting on the side of the road—apparently untamed by the fiery dust under him. A thin banana leaf mat was his only protection from the searing hot, baked sand.

Deciding to make a pit stop, Khadija and I perched ourselves next to the man and greeted him respectfully in Swahili. "*Shikamoo Baba,*" we whispered. His eyes, the darkest blue I have ever witnessed, opened wide at our voice. He was welcoming, sharing his only thin mat with us as we began to chat. I asked him if he would like some of our *maji* (water). He jumped at the opportunity, parched severely from the weather that blanketed the land.

For a few hours until the sun began to set, we would all sit and talk. What about? Anything really. We didn't need a topic. We didn't need to hand him a Gospel tract or tell him to shout hallelujah. What was our strategy? We had none. We simply desired to share in life together, even the hard and scorching times.

The older man looked worn and exhausted. It was outrageous what a little bottle of crisp, clean water would do. I attempted in my broken Swahili to communicate, constantly being interrupted by little Khadija's great language lessons. Her broken English and my broken Swahili made for a great pairing.

Sitting there in the dirt that day, I listened to the man's story. One that probably very few on the earth had ever asked him about. I wondered how many other stories of lives around the world had never been given a chance to be told. He relished in it, as if asked to speak at a large gathering. To him, his life was noble, and as he remembered more and more about his life, I watched a youthful glow and smile emerge across his weathered and wrinkled face.

What did I receive? Walking back that evening and dropping Khadija off at her hut, I told God, "If this is what the rest of my life could look like, I'd take it." One conversation was a defining twinkling of the eye that continued to launch my life into the oblivion of the unknown. I had met with Jesus again, only this time, I had to see behind the guise He had taken on.

> *I was hungry and you fed Me, I was thirsty and you gave Me a drink, I was homeless and you gave Me a room, I was shivering and you gave Me clothes, I was sick and you stopped to visit, I was in prison and you came to Me* (Matthew 25:34-36).

Cookie-Cutter Kids

We were not meant to be cookie-cutter people who mimic those we admire. We were meant to be unique—to break outside of the molds placed around us. We were created to be free. God offers us a life with no strings attached. A journey where the chains placed on us can no longer keep us held captive. It is a life where inhibitions and hesitations flee. It is much different from Western democratic thinking. The true cause of freedom is one that spans nations, crosses borders and boundaries, and unites us together in global liberation. True freedom is not a national agenda; it is a celestial promise and invasion.

I watch a lot of people trying so desperately to fit and squeeze themselves into the molds set before them. I attempted it myself. Remember? What would you do if I told you that you could break through the molds you've been placed in? What would your life look like if you threw them away and began running after what God has promised you? Would you break free from the molds and boxes placed around you?

Mary had a difficult time in her own life. There was no "pregnant with God" frame she could stuff herself into. She had no choice but to start from scratch and create that divine template with Heaven's help. It was met with reproach and disgrace from others.

When you decide to break free from the templates and the casts that others have put on you, there will be consequences. Your uncensored faith will often be met with misunderstanding and judgment. In the end, though, the fruit in your life will speak more words than you could ever attempt to explain on your own.

It is time for us to begin to reject control and live in the freedom that only Jesus can give. What would happen if we started living without the fear of condemnation or words from others? It is not a call to rebellion. This is a cry for freedom—one that will spread like wildfire if only a few will step out to lead the way in front of us. Your bravery could set others free. What would a life like that look like?

Hunger Is in the Air

Nearly a hundred people from all places on the globe were crammed closely together on the ground. Sweat was beading down our cheeks and as we were shoved up against each other. The small prayer hut seemed to take on the nature of a makeshift furnace. Children ran through in every direction, playing and attempting to skip in the midst of the compacted crowd. Why were we here? Why would we stay put in painfully forceful heat? We wanted to learn what it meant to be hungry for God. No pomp and circumstance. We wanted to see truth come in our lives without show and props.

Heidi had invited a small group of pastors from Mozambique—friends of hers who knew more about hunger than I could ever imagine. Each of them had had family members die from starvation. They knew hunger. And they pressed into Heaven like I have never before witnessed in my life. When they prayed, God came running. It was wild!

The newly formed group offered to pray over us to receive a gift of hunger. Coming from the background that I had, hunger was never an option in my life. There was never a worry. If anything, it was the very opposite. We often had too much!

Scuffling up front, Pastor Jose prayed over me, and as soon as he placed his hand on my head, I instantly found myself stuck face-first on the tile and grout and dust blowing in from the large gusts of wind surrounding us. What was happening? I was catching a gift that I couldn't possibly have found or made on my own. It was impossible for me to understand hunger, much less create or develop it. I needed help.

That day smashed against the ground was one of the defining moments that backed Randi and I in running after the promises inside of us. That kind of intense hunger knows no boundaries. It is a craving that disregards barriers to get to the source of its longing.

Along the Winding Road

The road I had traveled thus far was winding and unpaved. I had no idea where I was going at times or how I would get there, wherever "there" was. This way that God had opened for us was exhilarating and, at times, scary. There were days when I watched blind eyes pop open, moments when I watched hundreds and sometimes thousands run to Jesus with open arms. There were also waking hours filled with sadness, confusion, and hurt. Somehow all of these opposites existed together.

In the end—or should I say the beginning—they were all eclipsed by one look. How did we continue in the midst of times when Heaven seemed to flee instead of draw near? Why would we press into a road where we were constantly sick with malaria and unceasingly wondering where we would sleep next? As odd as it may sound, we found a love that we couldn't resist. It would overwhelm everything else when times got tough.

It was on my "yellow brick road" attempting to find the "land of Oz" that I realized with me were friends and family whom I had met along the way. In each continent, each country, each city, each village, and each home that we entered, we found gems—gifts—that we still treasure to this day. This journey is to be trudged together. It is in a place of family that we can keep running to the ends of the earth.

The "one-man show" in faith is fizzling out of existence. God is setting up an ancient and new prototype in the earth around us. He is not looking for lone prophets who go it alone. His heart is for teamwork—family. This is not a nameless, faceless generation. We all have faces and names, which He calls us by. Our desire is not for one person to be elevated. It is for companionship and joint efforts in pulling the Kingdom of God down to earth in cities around us.

Know That Place

So, how do we keep going in the midst of an unmarked road that beckons us to step on? What exactly is this "place" we have been mulling over in our conversation through these pages? This place is the location of living in God's heart, so much so that things change around you. What? No secret formula? I'm afraid not. It's the nitty-gritty reality of wrestling with Heaven in the messiness of our own lives—experiencing for ourselves what it looks like to see light encapsulate the darkness inch by inch.

Are you in love with Jesus? Has He captured your imagination? My friends, Heidi and Rolland Baker, know this place very well. They've built their home there. To them, our lives are all about seeing the face of Jesus.

Just focus on His face. You will only make it to the end if you can focus on His face. Focus on His beautiful face. You can't feed the poor, you can't go to the street, you can't see anything happen unless you see His face. One glance of His eyes, and we have all it takes to lie down.[1]

Where is this place of laid-down love located? The heartbeat of Jesus will guide you there. He's placed a spiritual GPS system in all of us to find it. He wants all of us.

His call is for our lives…He is looking for people who will carry His glory. He really, really is. But you have to be dead in order to carry it. And when you carry the glory, you will carry it out to the poor, the broken, the dying, and the lost. You will. That is the call. That is the heartbeat of Jesus, that we carry Him out to the broken. But you can't carry Him until you've seen His face. You have to know that holy place.[2]

Cling to Him

In a flash, He was gone. There she was, staring up into the Middle Eastern sky, wondering how long He would be gone before He would return again. The days that followed were full of contemplations—those same ponderings that kept her going throughout her life thus far. Mary sat in the rich red dirt once more and wondered about her life.

What did she do after Jesus ascended? Only one thing is written. Mary clung to Him with all of her might. What do you think Mary's journal would have looked like? She had experienced what it looked like to carry, birth, nurture, protect, and give up a new move in the earth that God asked her to be a part of. She was keenly aware of the death of her promise. And, in the end, she found out it was only the beginning.

Nearly two months later, Mary would undergo a final overshadowing of the Holy Spirit. A time where Heaven would not just hover over her and birth something through her, but make its home and dwell within her. She was called to carry Heaven into eternity.

As fire fell on each of them at Pentecost, Mary began to see that her promise had multiplied before her. In front of her, she touched a pledge that this movement would span generations and transcend who she was. Her obedience would touch many and open up a hidden path for millions to come. Mary's promise would outlive her and be continually carried by others who were not yet there.

We need to come face to face with the understanding of clinging to Jesus in both the death and the rebirth of our promises. The beat within us will be solidified in Him. He is our source of power, refilling, and renewal.

Mary and the others were told to wait for more power. They and we were given another promise of being constantly and continually filled up by Heaven's touch—God's presence in our lives. Are you full?

The infilling and baptism of the Holy Spirit is a daily process in our lives. Each day is a chance for us to encounter the One we live for. We no longer live for ourselves, but for the One who left the glory of Heaven just for us.

Receive

Constantly being refilled with the Holy Spirit's presence gives us fuel for the journey ahead. Believe me, you will need it! Before Jesus ascended into Heaven, He left those who loved Him with a couple gifts. One was peace. His peace would be unlike what they had experienced in the world around them.

Looking at them, Jesus got close one last time. He was so close that they could feel His breath. And without explanation, He blew on them! Breathing His breath, He said, "Receive the Holy Spirit. I am sending you now just as My Father sent Me. You are to do what I do. Got it?"

If I were one of the people there, I probably would have passed out cold on the floor! How could I possibly live a life that mirrored Jesus? Sure, we have managed to make it cute and cuddly looking for those we market it to. But the raw, uncensored version of His life was hard, rough, and downright brutal. How could I do that, Jesus?

That the Lamb would receive the reward for His suffering was the famous Moravian cry in the beginning of mission's history. We long to give up our lives as offerings to Jesus, as He did for us. But it isn't that easy. Jesus made it clear that we needed something that we were void of before we could start out on the dusty road ahead of us. He said we needed His Spirit—His breath.

We have to receive from Heaven so that Jesus will receive His reward through our lives. We cannot do it on our own. With even the greatest and most pure of intentions, we need His help. It's just that simple!

Hopefully during our journey together in these pages, you have begun to catch what it means to receive and grasp the give-and-take relationship of carrying Heaven around you. You have been called out for outrageous exploits under Heaven's shadow. Are you ready to receive?

Endnotes

1. Rolland Baker and Heidi Baker, *Always Enough: God's Miraculous Provision Among the Poorest Children on Earth* (Grand Rapids, MI: Chosen Books, 2003), 177.

2. Ibid., 178.

Chapter 13

His Reward

> *"That the Lamb would receive the reward for His suffering."*
> —The Moravian Missions Cry

I sat down one day—well, several days now—to write about a journey around the world. It was a trek that I was completely unprepared for, unaware of what would greet me on its footpath. At first, these pages were simple journal entries that I made over time. Soon, the realization came that this story transcended myself. It would become a shared story—a tale of a road packed with many others who carried the same heart and longing to meet with God and live life out of a remarkable relationship with Him. It is a place where you, too, have the choice to enter in.

In our conversation that we have begun together, I shared with you memories of the good, the bad, and the ugly faces of giving your life away to find a spiritual homeland in Jesus. Together, we journeyed through miracles, mud, and *much* mayhem. It has been a breathtaking ride. But I dare you to ask the question, "Where do we go from here?"

Many of us are searching for permission deep down to live a lifestyle that rejects everything we have been taught to attain—to go against the grain of the societies we live in and pursue a Kingdom upside down from life as we know it. From a cultural standpoint, leaving our identities in our nation, families, careers, or education is one of the most harrowing of decisions. When we cut ties that have kept us from who we have been created to be in fullness, things will get wobbly for a while. Relearning the basics of God's heart is both a frustrating and liberating initiative.

What does it take to cross the line that stands in front of us into this unpaved pathway? One step. That's all. It is the choice to step out and test the ground ahead of us.

What is your promise? Have you been able to hear it within you? Can you define it? What has God spoken to you? Whispered to you? Has your appetite been whetted by our journey? Then don't let it end here. Once we receive, we can give out. And that is my charge to you.

Mary did not let circumstances stop her. The reproach of carrying Heaven would stun her in the days to come, but her life is an outline for you and for me. Where are you on your journey? You might be in the place where you have begun to hear the whispers of Heaven about your life and your destiny. You might need to be overshadowed by God's presence to get you there. Have you met with Jesus? Or do you need to position yourself to encounter Him in fullness?

Some of you have said "yes" to the promises of God within your life. You've answered, and now the way has become more difficult than you signed up for in the beginning. Keep going. Through the valleys, know that they will soon be built up into mountain highs. Trust me, they won't stop there!

Still others of you have felt the painful sting of the death of your promise. You have given your life for something—all that you were—only to see it come to life in the world around you. And suddenly and without warning, it was gone. You find yourself stuck in the waiting and holding on for dear life. Stick with it. For mourning always converges into joy. Death cannot stay there. Your promise can be revived! What were you promised in the beginning? Grab onto it and call it back to life.

Step out of your comfort zone, wherever you are, and ask God to reveal Himself to you. Ask Him to share with you His heart for your life. It doesn't mean that you will jump on a plane and head to Africa to find it, although some of you will. Listen for that heartbeat inside of you and follow it where it leads.

Healing in the Hut and the Hotel

Just the other day, I was ministering at a healing service in Ohio. It lasted for nearly five hours, and not one person who came in sick left unhealed. Everyone was healed! I had never experienced a time when that occurred—when not one sickness remained. Four minutes into the meeting, a man's knee, which needed a replacement that he couldn't afford, was completely restored. The man began running through the church like it was a racetrack! Knees were being healed. Back injuries of all kinds were healed. Two women who had partial and complete blindness were healed! Whole body arthritis was suddenly gone! A neck injury was completely healed. A sciatic nerve problem was instantly healed with no pain. A woman with multiple sclerosis was healed and could do things she hadn't been able to do in years. Depression was completely obliterated, and many who struggled with nightmares and insomnia were completely delivered.

People were filled with the Holy Spirit for the first time. And people were instantaneously being released to flow in the prophetic ministry, hearing God's heart on behalf of others with no previous knowledge or training of what it was! People were not just spectators. They took ownership in participating in the move that was taking place.

God's fire was being poured out all over the place. People felt heat to the point where they opened the doors to let the cold, 35 degree Fahrenheit weather rush in…but it didn't work. The fire of the Holy Spirit was present and healing so many.

People were getting so filled with the joy of the Holy Spirit that they were unable to sit or stand. The most amazing part was that this group of people had no grid for healing or the presence of God in this capacity. They had no training but were hungry.

It doesn't matter what your background is—what your cultural upbringing has shown and instilled in you. When the real presence of God invades our lives, we know it is real. It means that we have a choice to enter into what God is doing around us.

A Love-Struck Nomad

Will we go anywhere to meet with God? Can we hear the call? Can we hear His heart's cry? It shatters realms just to reach us. Take all we are, Jesus. What does a life poured out look like? God's presence is what we live for. I crave His presence. It's the very air we breathe. It's life to us. It awakens us. His presence is where it all began for me, in the dirt that unexpected day in Africa's heart.

What can people learn from my story—the journal of a young woman who dove into the third world and somehow and unexpectedly met with God? As simple as it might sound, if I can do it in my little, uncoordinated life, you can as well. I didn't find a golden ticket to get there. But I determined to get to a place of living out of the reality of meeting with Jesus each day.

Diving to the Depths of Love

I can remember, before ever setting out on our journey, meeting with Lesley-Anne Leighton, a fiery Kiwi woman from New Zealand. She left me with a tenacity and boldness that disregarded judgment and misunderstanding from others.

Sitting with her in a little clay room in a little plastic Coca-Cola chair, I began sharing with her my encounter with Jesus on the shore the very night before setting out on my journey. The moment when, under the moonlight path, He asked me to step out and trust Him on a journey of endless proportions.

Looking at me in her usual understanding way, Lesley stared into my eyes and said, "Go for it, honey!" Her reaction shocked me. Her affirmations blew my mind. Most people would have told me to go back to America and raise a pocketful of money, buy the latest of mosquito repellant, and throw a couple granola bars in my suitcase before leaving. They would give me a list of *to-dos* in hopes of helping me. However, sometimes our methods become distractions to the timing of Heaven.

But there she was, enthralled by what God had been whispering to me. Lesley stuck her small hands on my shoulders and began to pray over me, calling out what she saw God showing her about my life. We both ended up on the cold, dirt floor in minutes.

Stuck on the floor for hours, God packed my "suitcase" with supplies I could get nowhere but from Him. Lesley began to prophesy over me as I was shaking under God's presence there, face pressed against the side of the Coca-Cola chair that used to hold me. She saw homes for rescued children being erected throughout the earth, beginning with Africa. She was calling out the end in the beginning for my life. Little did Lesley know that God would show me that children were His promise to me in nations throughout the earth. As I see the nearing of those homes being built in Africa, I can hear her words and laughter echoing through my memory.

I would end up learning from Lesley side by side as I traveled with her in months to follow. Looking back, I am reminded of the significance of that day and those hours helplessly smashed together with the African dust.

Remaining in His Gaze

It is now our turn to carry Heaven. The ponderings that Mary treasured within her heart remained and lived after her promise was fulfilled. As her life flashed before her eyes, she was reminded of the road she had walked through so many ups and downs. Sitting here writing, my own odyssey began reeling through my eyes as well. In it, I saw again each step where I had been. It was our journeys and memories through good times and bad. There were times when I met with Jesus on my face. The realization that He had given us a life of such wonder and amazement was an incomprehensible and lasting gift.

Our adventures continue. Talking on the phone with Randi last night, we wondered where God would send us next. Deliberating together, we asked each other if we would continue to say "yes" to the road ahead, full of just as many unknowns as the way behind us.

What about you? Will you continue to say "yes" to what God has placed inside of you? To the pathway set before you? No matter what part of the street you find yourself on, what is your cry?

The Margins Compel Us

As the Range Rover's tires became caked with the mud beneath it, splatters of debris from the wet and sopping ground shot through the air, landing in our hair and on our faces. Sharing a set of earphones, *The Lion King* soundtrack was blaring in our ears. We had been given a gift of a safari in East Africa. As the song, "The Circle of Life," lyrically rang through the warm tropical air, we could see it. It was a promise of a group of people walking the road with us. It was a promise of full life—a rallying of those who shared the same hunger to go after their promises together. You are one of those we caught a glimpse of that afternoon.

This tribe is simply an organism, one that is full of the living, breathing reality of the substance of Heaven on the earth. We are a family—a community seeking to seek out the thirsty, compel the poor, and rescue the hidden. In this process of learning to live, love, and walk as Jesus did, we are seeing with new eyes those who hunger and thirst in front of us and in the world.

Before I hopped on a plane headed to Africa when I was 18, I thought that my job was to bring Jesus into the entire world. Remember when I told you I was surprised that He was already there when my plane landed? It's true. He is waiting for us in the midst of the world to find Him and join in with His heart for the people we go to. It is a choice to live, love, and learn on the margins, one day at a time.

Jesus spent most of His time on earth with the marginalized—those who were separated from society as a whole. The people on the margins, the poor, became those He would call friends and His family. He now calls us to join those on the margins by coming out and being separate as well. Hidden within the naked reality of the God who came to the earth as a babe in the dirt was the overwhelming picture of Heaven dancing with the earth. We long to see the same, one person at a time.

Carriers of Heaven

Do you want God just to show up with angels in a village, a city, or a nation? Or do you want to learn to sit one day at a time and learn both suffering and joy? This process makes us childlike. There are lots of things about your call that may not make sense. But God doesn't do it our way. He is looking for yielded lovers who are so in love that they do not care what it costs or what it looks like!

He doesn't want us to receive our promise and purpose and then let it die. He wants you to bring it to full term. He asks you to nurture it as a mother nurtures her child. She waits for that child. For the joy set before her, she carries the child to full term. She blesses it. In good times and in bad, she stands firm in love.

You were meant to carry Heaven. The Christian life was never intended to find its culmination in mass crowds of people glued to padded benches. If you want more from life than sitting in a church pew, then this promise is for you.

Just Dance

Stepping into His big shoes again, I saw myself in a flowing dress. Jesus walked up to me in a robe. It wasn't a royal robe, but a poor man's robe. Without a word, He put His hand out again, inviting me to dance with Him. The last picture I saw was my hand in His, stepping together barefoot into the realm of garbage dumps, poverty, and hunger.

As our feet touched the dirt, the ground around us was transformed. In front of me was a Kingdom that was once hidden, but in reality had been there the entire time. He had kept His promise. I would see the rebirth of His heartbeat within me unveiled in the faces of the poor, one small child at a time.

These were my first baby steps into an upside-down Kingdom in the dirt. As I glanced at the muddy road in front of me, my eyes stretched to the end of the horizon. I had just begun. As I looked again, I could see His large bare footprints engraved in the path before me. There was much more in the trail ahead. He would show me the way, one step at a time.

Echoes Through Time

In Herrnhut, Germany, on August 13, 1727, one of the most profound and impacting prayers was emitted. Its magnitude was not in creative wording, but in the movement that its breath ignited.

These words created prayers unbroken for 100 years; their echoes still felt today, provided the modern Church with the first missions movement and an unyielding benchmark for the true passion and power of fervent prayer.[1]

They were known as the Moravians. It was a community of radicals who committed their lives to knowing Jesus and making Him famous in the nations. Only 48 young Christians comprised the growing tribe.

A slave escaped from a Caribbean sugarcane island and, by divine providence, met Zinzendorf—the leader of the Moravian movement—in Vienna. In the wake of this encounter, two men from the Moravian community dedicated themselves to bringing the Gospel to the slave island. Their names were John Leonard Dover, a potter, and David Niechmann, a carpenter. They were both only 19 years old. In order to get onto the island, John and David had to sell themselves into slavery. The money raised from their sale began the Moravian missions fund. As the two men stood at the dock, John's family tried to dissuade him from leaving—moments before setting sail, John Leonard Dober voiced what was to become the Moravian battle cry: *"I do this that the Lamb may receive the reward for His suffering."*[2]

Their echoes are still felt today.... God is raising up a new generation. The same vow that inspired Zinzendorf's community remains today. God's commission has no expiry date. The momentum created by the passion of the early missionaries cannot simply fade to gray. In a society enamored with the preservation of self, the echoes of the Moravians are beginning to stir once again; none live for themselves.

This is the call of a new generation—it began then and still remains—that we would live with that same zeal—count our lives as forfeit for the sake of the Gospel. It is a passion fueled by the absolute courage of Christ's victory. It is a generation founded in abandoned prayer and worship. It is the outworking of community and missions. It is sacrifice and destiny.

Those who answer the call will make echoes of their own, not for their achievements, fame, or their household names, but because they choose to respond to the ageless vow of the Moravians and give their lives away.

"…that the Lamb may receive the reward for His suffering."[3]

A Holy Charge

When Jesus strolled back into the town He was raised in, He was given a holy charge in front of all who knew Him.

> *Unrolling the scroll, He found the place where it was written, God's Spirit is on Me; He's chosen Me to preach the Message of good news to the poor, sent Me to announce pardon to prisoners and recovery of sight to the blind, to set the burdened and battered free, to announce, "This is God's year to act!" He rolled up the scroll, handed it back to the assistant, and sat down. Every eye in the place was on Him, intent. Then He started in, "You've just heard Scripture make history. It came true just now in this place"* (Luke 4:17-20).

This same charge is one that echoes through our lives in this day.

Before heading out, Heidi and Lesley prayed over Randi and me. Their words still ring throughout my mind. The charge they sent us out into the world with was simple and strong. It was a holy pledge that we chose to live our life by, one day at a time. I would like to send you out with the same charge. Are you ready to be sent out from His face? God, You left Heaven. Surely we can leave our place—where we are at in our lives—to find more of You.

As God sent Jesus into the world, Jesus is sending *you* into the world.

You are not alone. The Spirit of the Lord is on you to preach good news to the poor. He has sent you to proclaim freedom for prisoners and recovery of sight for the blind, to release the oppressed, to proclaim the year of the Lord's favor.

Will you proclaim the good news of the Kingdom? Will you heal the sick and raise the dead? Will you cleanse those who have leprosy and drive out demons?

Daily will you take up your cross and follow Jesus? Will you Love the Lord your God with all your soul and mind? And will you love your neighbor as yourself? (See Matthew 22:37-39.)

Will you love the poor, the widow, the orphan, and the unlovely through the action of "downward mobility"[4] in word, sign, and deed? Will you go into the streets and alleys of the world and bring in the poor, the crippled, the blind, and the lame and invite them to the banquet that His house may be full?

As Jesus said these words to His followers, Jesus is also saying them to you:

> *Therefore go and make disciples of all nations, baptizing them in the name of the Father and of the Son and of the Holy Spirit, and teaching them to obey everything I have commanded you. And surely I am with you always, to the very end of the age* (Matthew 28:19-20 NIV).

Go! Go! Go![5]

Our message remains simple—love the one in front of you. And this is what we will set our hearts to do. All that we are is given for all of Him.

Called Forth

Before Mary was "Mary, the mother of Jesus," she was just a simple girl minding her own business in her own little closed-in world. She might not have been aiming for the life that she was thrown into—perhaps it just wasn't her ambition. But it *was* who she was deep inside.

Each one of you reading these words has been chosen and called forth. You have this radical destiny in God. Will you say "yes"? Is there a "yes" cry in your heart? Is there a "yes" to the cost, a "yes" to the suffering, and a "yes" to the joy that will come inside of you?

Nothing is impossible with God.

"I am the Lord's servant," Mary said. Are you? Can you say with Mary, "God, may it be to me as You have said"? Can those words be found true inside you?

You are not alone, and God is lifting up many who are seeking a similar homeland—a place where Heaven touches earth with power. Mary's life is an invitation and mirror into a life of carrying Heaven and birthing the promises placed in our lives.

Your journey may look a little different from mine, but the destination is always the same. If you are hungry for a life where God lives in and through you, forget the strategies and hoops that have been placed in front of you. The entrance around back remains swung open for you and me to enter into an upside-down Kingdom where the hungry always get fed.

There is a certainty in the promises placed within your life. In Hebrews, God solidifies His intentions and commitment for the long haul in each of our everyday lives.

> *When God made His promise to Abraham, since there was no one greater for Him to swear by, He swore by Himself, saying, "I will surely bless you and give you many descendents." And so after waiting patiently, Abraham received what was promised. …Because God wanted to make the unchanging nature of His purpose very clear to the heirs of what was promised, He confirmed it with an oath. God did this so that, by two unchangeable things in which it is impossible for God to lie, we who have fled to take hold of the hope offered to us may be greatly encouraged. We have this hope as an anchor for the soul, firm and secure. It enters the inner sanctuary behind the curtain, where Jesus, who went before us, has entered on our behalf…* (Hebrews 6:13-20 NIV).

Mary positioned herself to partner with God to bring about a new move of the Spirit in the world around her—to bring about Jesus, who made a way for us to connect with the Father in an outrageous way. Mary's promise was a gateway for us to team up with Jesus to bring about a greater movement of the Holy Spirit than the world had ever before witnessed.

We've been invited to step into the promises of God for our lives, but also to jump into already-paved paths that have been marked by those who have gone before us. One connection with Heaven changed Mary's life and the world around her forever. What about you? Are you ready for your own run-in with destiny? It's time to take hold of the promises in your life and watch the world around you shake from the aftershocks of your own meeting with God. It all began with a simple "yes!"

His question echoes through all of time. What is *your* heart's cry?

Endnotes

1. Taken with permission from the jacket of "Receive," sung by Cindy Ruakere.

2. http://www.watchword.org/index.php?option=com_content&task=view&Itermid=48.

3. Taken with permission from the jacket of "Receive," sung by Cindy Ruakere.

4. Dr. Rene Padilla, International President, Tearfund International, www.tearfund.org.

5. Taken with permission from Lesley-Anne Leighton, Director, Holy Given International School of Missions, www.holygiven.org.

About Jessica J. Davis

Jessica is actively involved in mobilizing a supernatural justice movement worldwide. Her heart beats with a passion to see people embrace the Person of Love and His embodiment in the earth. Jessica and her husband, Joshua, direct Awaken, Inc. She is a graduate of Campbellsville University, The Iris Holy Given International School of Missions, and The MorningStar University. She is ordained by Iris Ministries and has ministered in over 20 countries. Jessica's life message affirms that the Gospel is and will forever remain simple—love the one in front of you.

www.awakenworldwide.org

www.Jessicajdavis.com

www.joshandjessdavis.com

www.ALifeOvershadowed.com

In the right hands, This Book will Change Lives!

Most of the people who need this message will not be looking for this book. To change their lives, you need to put a copy of this book in their hands.

> *But others (seeds) fell into good ground, and brought forth fruit, some a hundred-fold, some sixty-fold, some thirty-fold* (Matthew 13:8).

Our ministry is constantly seeking methods to find the good ground, the people who need this anointed message to change their lives. Will you help us reach these people?

> *Remember this—a farmer who plants only a few seeds will get a small crop. But the one who plants generously will get a generous crop* (2 Corinthians 9:6).

EXTEND THIS MINISTRY BY SOWING
3 BOOKS, 5 BOOKS, 10 BOOKS, OR MORE TODAY, AND BECOME A LIFE CHANGER!

Thank you,

Don Nori Sr., Publisher
Destiny Image
Since 1982